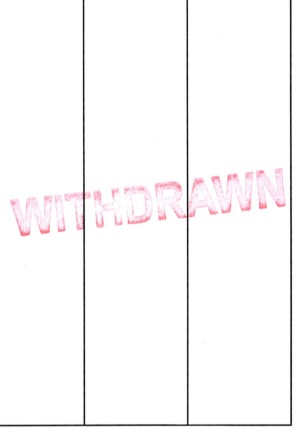

# Intimacy or Integrity

## PHILOSOPHY AND CULTURAL DIFFERENCE

The 1998 Gilbert Ryle Lectures

*Thomas P. Kasulis*

UNIVERSITY OF HAWAI'I PRESS

HONOLULU

**Library of Congress Cataloging-in-Publication Data**
Kasulis, Thomas P.
  Intimacy or integrity : philosophy and cultural difference /
Thomas P. Kasulis.
    p. cm.
  "The 1998 Gilbert Ryle lectures."
  Includes bibliographical references and index.
  ISBN 0–8248–2476–8 (cloth) — ISBN 0–8248–2559–4 (pbk.)
    1. Integrity.  2. Intimacy (Psychology).  3. Culture—
Philosophy.  I. Title.
  BJ1533.I58 K38 2002
  179'.9—dc21

                             2001058303

University of Hawai'i Press books are printed on acid-free
paper and meet the guidelines for permanence and
durability of the Council on Library Resources

*Printed by The Maple-Vail Book Manufacturing Group*

*For Benedict, Matthias, and Telemachus*

# CONTENTS

**ACKNOWLEDGMENTS**

The ideas behind this book have been percolating for some time, at least fifteen or twenty years. It is even harder than usual, therefore, to give appropriate thanks to everyone contributing to this process in some way. There is no doubt, however, that this book would never have come into existence in its present form had it not been for the Philosophy Department at Trent University, which invited me to deliver the 1998 Gilbert Ryle Lectures. The lectures not only gave me the opportunity to give full articulation to my theories on the relation between thought and culture, but also forced me to think through matters in a more systematic and thorough way than I had ever done before. When my friend and colleague Robert E. Carter initially approached me about the lectures, I was pleased to accept. After my four lectures at Trent, I became all the more grateful for the privilege. Trent University has established a wonderful philosophical community of scholars and students. I benefited much from their insightful comments as well as their gracious hospitality.

Based on what I had learned from the response to the lectures, I rewrote them into a book manuscript that I shared with graduate students in an interdisciplinary seminar at the Ohio State University in the Division of Comparative Studies. The students in that course, some philosophers but most not, helped me see the ramifications of my theory, thereby instigating still further revisions and elaborations. Patricia Crosby, editor at the University of Hawai'i Press, showed enthusiastic interest in the project and shepherded the book to publication. I asked Pat whether Don Yoder, the copy editor for my *Zen Action/Zen Person*, could be enlisted to work on this manuscript and he kindly agreed. It had been two decades since I last worked with him. I knew I had become a better writer in the interim, but Don proved again he is still way ahead of me.

Over the years of experimenting with the theories in this book, I have found it increasingly valuable to use diagrams. Anne Mischo of Ohio

State's Information Services Department converted my scribblings into publishable form. I am grateful for the care and expedition she brought to the task.

For years this project has been developing in the background to what I thought I was doing in my research at the time, so I never sought any funding for it. Yet over the past decade or two, grants from the National Endowment for the Humanities, the American Council of Learned Societies, the Japan Foundation, and the Ohio State University have supported other projects that fertilized the ideas coming to fruition here. The same applies to those who have attended my lectures over the same period—my students, participants in National Endowment for the Humanities Summer Institutes and Seminars I have directed, and audiences of various sorts around the world. Sometimes they have unknowingly helped me in this project without saying a word. A mere look of consternation, boredom, or confusion would be enough to alert me that I needed a different example, a new diagram, another analogy, or a clearer expression. Five people in particular have encouraged me for years to write up my theory in a formal way: Robert Bellah, Roger T. Ames, Lloyd H. Steffen, Maryanna Klatt, and Nikki Bado-Fralick. Without their persistent questioning about my progress in bringing the theory to publication, I doubt if the topic would have been so much on my mind when I accepted the invitation to deliver the Ryle Lectures.

Finally, I want to thank my family. Philosophical thinking is always a solitary act, but my family has kept it from being lonely. My wife, Ellen, has endured my endless ruminations about what I was trying to do as a scholar and why. All the while, she has been patient and supportive, even if on occasion it meant feigning interest in yet further ramblings. My three sons—Benedict, Matthias, and Telemachus—are all adults now. Over the years, they have had to put up with my absences, either physical or intellectual, as I engaged in thinking through the theories of the kind discussed in this book. The last time I formally acknowledged my children in a book, Benedict was not yet born. I guess he was waiting for this one. I am sorry it took so long.

INTIMACY OR INTEGRITY

# INTRODUCTION

*"Kasurisu-san! Kasurisu-san!"* Mrs. Tani's call of my name carried up the stairs to my quarters in the rooming house. I knew by her tone that something was up—that she was having some problem with the folks downstairs and I was being summoned to mediate. The first level of her guest house was reserved for short-term tourists visiting Kyoto, and the living arrangements there resembled a youth hostel. The roomers were usually divided between Japanese and foreigners. Though Mrs. Tani's English was quite functional, problems sometimes arose that she referred to the resident graduate student of comparative philosophy. So I was called down from my room.

When I got to the large room where guests tended to congregate, I found three adults: one Japanese man and an American couple, all around thirty years old. They were agitated, upset, nearing a state of rage. There was also an eighteen-month-old girl in the room, obviously the child of the couple. She seemed calm, but most curious about the consternation around her.

As I began to sort out what had happened, I realized that the Japanese man spoke English quite well and that the problem had nothing to do with translation. Furthermore, the accounts offered by the Japanese man and the couple were virtually identical. So the problem was neither linguistic nor a disagreement over facts. Yet all three were deeply upset, the couple siding against the Japanese man and vice versa.

1

According to their accounts, I am confident the events were as follows. The little girl had been fascinated by the man's shiny wristwatch and he took it off his wrist to show her. She took it in her hand and smiled in glee, all the time looking up at the Japanese man who was smiling back. She dangled the watch in her hand, watching the reaction of the smiling man. She waved the watch more vigorously and the man still smiled. Finally, she winged the watch across the room, hitting the wall and breaking the crystal. Because the parents thought their child and the man had been getting along, they had not been paying much attention until they heard the clunk of the watch hitting the wall, accompanied by the little girl's giggle and the gasp of the Japanese man. Infuriated, the Japanese man wanted an apology and expected an offer to pay for the damage. The American couple responded that they had nothing to apologize for—in fact, it was the man's own fault. Why hadn't he said "no!" to the girl when she starting shaking the watch? The man rejoined that the couple must be bad parents: the child shouldn't have to be told "no." If they had been good parents, the child would have known it was wrong to throw the watch. She should have known that the man had given it to her to look at, not to throw.

I tried to intervene by explaining that children are raised differently in Japan and much of the West, especially countries like the United States. Japanese children are kept close to the mother at all times, often carried on the mother's back with the child facing forward. They learn to observe from a vantage point alongside the mother's face, thereby becoming acute onlookers of events in sync with the mother's responses. American children, by contrast, learn by exploring on their own. They engage in a tactile manipulation of the world, freely exploring their surroundings until restricted by an adult's intervention. The American baby learns that doing anything is okay until someone in authority says "no!" or obstructs its activity in some other way. Even though I had tried to explain all this, it was one of my least successful interventions. Each side continued to think there was something wrong or crazy about how the other had acted and what the other's analysis had been.

---

I lay in the hospital bed in the middle of the night, about a week after bilateral knee replacement surgery. The pain woke me and I buzzed the nurse's station to ask when I'd get my next dose of painkiller. Apparently I had a half hour to go. I stared at the ceiling, counting the minutes, trying to block out the pain, but I became increasingly uncomfortable. John, a night nurse, came into the room after a few minutes to check on me. He could see I was agitated. "It's getting nasty, isn't it, Tom?" "It's bad—both a crushing and stabbing pain." From experience, John also knew it was going to get much worse over the next several minutes. He sat down next to the bed and started chatting. Knowing my interest in East Asia, he shared with me some of his experiences training in kung fu. I told a couple of tales myself from my summer of aikido training in Japan. I managed a smile or two as we swapped "war stories." After about fifteen minutes, he got up and said he had to go get my medication. The time had passed quickly and while the pain had gotten intense, I had felt less anguish over it while I was talking.

The next morning a physician on rounds came in with a group of five or six medical students. When he asked how I was doing, I said I was "hanging in there." But I also mentioned that my sleep had been interrupted twice during the night because the painkiller had worn off. He checked his charts and read aloud (as much to the med students as to me) the medication and dosage. He then went on: "At this point in the patient's treatment, the regimen calls for a decrease in analgesic dosage to inhibit the likelihood of dependency. So, Mr. Kasulis (turning to me), I'm afraid there's nothing we can do about that right now. The prognosis is that in a few days you should be feeling better. Any questions?"

Later in the evening, I saw John again and told him about my morning visitation. With a smirk he said that doctors could act that way sometimes. "They have their rules and guidelines for treatment and that doc in particular goes by the book. Sometimes it seems he treats the disease and forgets about the patient. Anyway, don't worry. We'll get through this fine. And if things get out of hand tonight, I can contact the doctor on call to see if we can increase the dose a bit." With John's assurance and the knowledge that I had extra help if I really needed it, I was able to get through the night without extra medication. And after that, it did get better.

---

In many obvious respects, the two situations—separated in my life by a quarter century—were as different as could be. One took place in Kyoto, the other in Ohio. One involved people with different native languages, one with only native English-speakers. One had to do with dissimilarities in childrearing; the other involved a difference in medical care. One had to do with a contrast between people of different cultures and the other...well...the other had to do with a contrast between people of different cultures or at least subcultures. The disparity between my nurse and physician was as much a culture gap as that between the Japanese man and the American couple. In their analysis and response to my pain—both linguistically and behaviorally—the nurse and the doctor had functioned differently. For John, I was a person in pain and he took the time to come into my world, including its pain. For that fifteen minutes, John shared my moment of pain as much as we shared our martial arts experiences. He told me "we" would get through it and I trusted him *affectively* to be there for me. The doctor, of course, was also helping me deal with the pain by prescribing the necessary medication. But he seemed to be treating not me but the pain, simultaneously explaining medical principles to his students. When he said "we" could no nothing, I presumed he meant "we doctors." As almost a footnote to his treatment, he told me "you" would be feeling better. I trusted him, too. But it was a different kind of trust than my trust in John. I *intellectually* trusted the doctor's medical knowledge to explain and manage what was happening to me. The difference in these two kinds of trust reflects a difference in how the two medical practitioners analyzed my situation, communicated with me, and persuaded me that I had nothing to worry about. It really does amount to a cultural difference.

Although the content and even the context at the Kyoto rooming house and the Ohio hospital were radically unalike, the issues of analysis, communication, and persuasion were not all that different. Of course, the differences between the Japanese man and the American couple or between the nurse and the physician undoubtedly included individual personality traits and not just cultural disparity. Let us focus, however, on the cultural aspects. In very general terms, Japanese tend to raise their children to be responsive (coordinating oneself to the behavior and concerns of others), Americans to be responsible (to act freely within defined limits); the Japanese to be situational, the Americans to be rule-governed; the Japanese to value an affective intuition, the Americans to value cognitive "objectivity"; and so forth. In the hospital case, the physician embodies the values of scientifically objective data. In a detached way he uses the regimen developed out of statistical analysis without taking into consideration the idiosyncrasies of the case. The physician may have personality traits that make this form of behavior feel natural for him, but he was probably acculturated into these patterns—as indeed he is acculturating the next generation of medical students on rounds with him. Meanwhile, if nurses in training were under John's tutelage they would learn how to be responsive to the situation, how to enter into the patient's experience (in my case the East Asian martial arts) for resources, how to sense what the patient is *not* saying.

I am not trying to make any essential claims at this point about Japanese and American culture or the training of nurses and physicians. It would be reckless to do so on the basis of two anecdotes. Even if my expansive generalizations had within them a quality of truth, they would be useless without some sensitivity to counterevidence and exceptions. I am simply suggesting that when comparing cultures in terms of their similarities and differences, we might find it helpful to watch for certain general patterns that might have heuristic value. This will aid our concern for the possibilities and limitations of cross-cultural analysis, communication, and cooperation.

In the context of this book, as my second anecdote suggests, the term "culture" is broadly construed to include not only national cultures, such as Japanese culture, American culture, or German culture, but also subcultures within these national cultures and even subcultures that may cut across national cultures—subcultures marked, for example, by gender, economic or social class, ethnicity, or various forms of the altern or subaltern. With respect to the prospect for crossing the boundaries separating such cultures or subcultures, we commonly find either of two opposing assumptions. Each contains some truth but taken alone is too limiting. On the one hand is the presumption that we are living in an increasingly globalized context where cultural differences can be recognized and negotiated via the universal acceptance of common values. The present call for an international recognition of "human rights" is of this sort: whatever the differences among us might be, the assumption is that if we can agree on a few basic universal ideas, mutually beneficial cooperation will follow. On the other hand, there are those who resist such globalizing as a threat to culturally meaningful difference and diversity. Instead of universalization, such cultural critics expect or endorse a manifold of liaisons among people of similar background, experience, values, or interests. Marxism's "class consciousness" arose from such a model, as do many other forms of racial, ethnic, and gendered forms of self-identification or solidarity. Often the assumption is that those-who-are-not-us can never understand who we are, so we should never allow "them" to define, interpret, or categorize us. The argument is that cooperation, if indeed it is actually possible, should not arise from the oppressive homogenization that universal structures either wittingly or unwittingly support. Instead, the claim is that cooperation should arise from some community of conversation in which people of different worldviews strive together for common goals.

It is in this world of simultaneous globalization and balkanization that I live as a philosopher who has spent his career studying both Western and Asian traditions. I have sympathies with both the universalists and the differentialists. But I also believe they tend to forge their fundamental insights into fanatical positions lacking justification. The extreme universalists fail to appreciate how profound cultural difference can be. For instance, they may confuse the superficial acceptance of foreign terminology with the actual acceptance of foreign values. To cite one instance, the Japanese equivalent of the English word "rights" is *"kenri."* Invented to translate the newly introduced Western term, the term has been part of the Japanese vocabulary for about a century. The Japanese people generally understand quite well to what the term *"kenri"* refers, and its presence in the language may suggest to a universalist that Japan is in accord with liberal democratic principles. Yet the sense and use of the term *"kenri"*—its force, its normative functions, its relation to other key notions or values, its use in argument—are not the same as for the English word "rights." When in America I probably use, read, or hear the term "rights" in ordinary contexts several times a day. When in Japan, however, the word *"kenri"* may not come up for days at a time. The presence of the word *"kenri"* in the Japanese language exemplifies the kind of phenomenon that the universalist—eagerly seeking common ground wherever possible—may easily misinterpret. The transfer of words or even ideas from one culture to the next does not entail a shared cultural view of what is important.

The extreme differentialists, by contrast, may cavalierly ignore that communication and understanding often cross the boundaries of otherness. Translation is possible. Indeed the wartime British and American cryptologists could not only translate Japanese messages but could do so even when they were written in a code explicitly designed to befuddle Japan's enemies. So at least sometimes one can understand the "other," even if the other does not want that person to be able to do so. Furthermore, even to claim "they" can never really understand "us" assumes we understand the other well enough to know her or his capacity to understand us. Without some understanding across boundaries, the very claim about the impossibility of universalizing is itself a universalization.

In trying to think through what is right and wrong about the universalist and differentialist positions, it occurred to me that there was a blurring of the distinction between understanding and persuasion. We might understand the other (the universalists are right on this count), but we are not necessarily persuaded by or sympathetic to the other (the differentialists are right on this count). In fact, the boundaries separating cultures or subcultures are often most visible when we understand what the other is saying but do not grasp its relevance. When one side accuses the other of not listening, the criticism sometimes means that one does not *care* to understand. In saying "you are irrational," the criticism is not so much "you are wrong" as "you're missing the point." When I am crossing a cultural boundary—for example, in visiting a country where the people and I share no common language—I may feel quite alone. The alienation is much deeper, however, when the people and I share a language but what I argue is totally unpersuasive or what I explicate receives nothing more than a puzzled look. In this case, the alienation is not simply "they are like me but speak a different language" (something a good translator can fix). Instead, it is the profound sense of alienation and difference of the sort "they are not like me at all." Such a strong sense of otherness cannot be fixed by a simple translation. The boundary does not prevent understanding in the technical sense; instead it undermines trust, the basis of any complex accord.

Often the lack of cross-cultural agreement is not over this idea or that argument, but over something more holistic. The gap between the interlocutors is such that each missed not a particular point but the whole picture. This recognition led me to the unsettling conclusion that if I were, for example, to teach my American students about Japanese culture, I somehow had to compare *all* of American and *all* of Japanese culture. This was worrisome on two counts. First, such a holistic comparison could not possibly do justice to the complexity, richness, and diversity within each culture. Generalizations are always distortions. Yet what articulation is not a distortion of some sort? Besides, even the most rudimentary analysis of human thought reveals that generalization is a common—and inevitable—aspect of many learning situations. Generalizations come first; then, with further study, one discovers the exceptions, the nuances, and the qualifications. Without the generalization, however, people cannot proceed in their quest for understanding anymore than they can use most databases without first defining the fields of entry. Generalization is a necessary part of organization. A generalization is not the same as a universal qualifier: a generalization cannot be refuted by a simple counterexample. A generalization, by its very nature, always has exceptions. The only way to refute a generalization is by posing a better generalization (one that is a more effective heuristic, one that can account for more of the data, or whatever). Indeed, to say no generalization is accurate is itself to make a generalization (or, even worse, a universalization). Accepting these ground rules, I decided to live and work with generalization as the inevitable first step to deeper insight.

The second sticking point about comparing cultures or subcultures holistically was that an analysis of either whole would seem to be infinite. Doing *two* infinite analyses for the sake of comparison was hardly an improvement. It seems the more detailed and rich the analysis, the more impossible a true comparison becomes. Consider two diagrammatic representations of a tree (Figure 1). Are they the same or different? At first glance, they seem different but yet, somehow, also similar. The differences resemble variations among individual trees of the same species.

If we look more closely, though, the particularity of each tree begins to emerge. In fact, if we zoom in on a comparable sector of each tree (for example, the top section just left of center) we get the configurations shown in Figure 2. Imagine trying to make a comparison between the two trees on this level! They seem so different that it is hard even to make a generality for comparison. If we cannot compare even these small sections of the tree, how could an attempt to compare the whole trees do anything but fail? An adequate analysis would seem to take forever. And

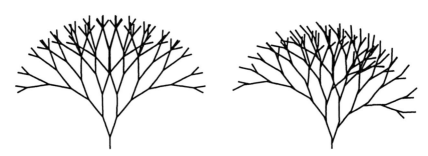

FIGURE 1. Two Trees

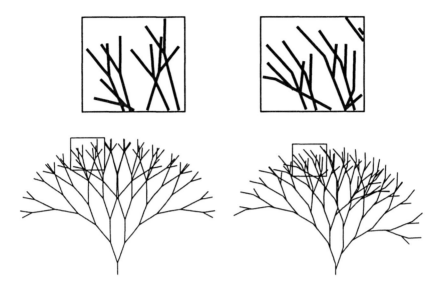

FIGURE 2. Close-ups of Parts of Two Trees

once done (at least to a point where we quit), we would literally lose the forest for the trees—the initial sense of similarity would all but disappear. This is much like the problem of comparing cultures: superficial similarity, upon closer analysis, dissolves into incomparables and difference.

Before surrendering to this analysis, however, let us look more closely at the very ends of the branches on the two trees in Figure 1. Within each tree, the branch tips are all the same; but compared to the other tree, they are different. There is a remarkable consistency within each tree—every branch ends in the same way—but each tree displays a different pattern of consistency. Now let us look at the tree trunks at their very base, where their trunks first begin to split off. Again the two trees differ somewhat, but they do so in exactly the same way as the branch tips. Finally, let us go back and look at the whole two trees together. The first tree is exactly symmetrical—symmetrical in the same way as its branch tips— whereas the other displays the overall shape of its own tiniest branch ends. The cat is now out of the bag. Each tree is generated from the recursive duplication or reiteration of a simple three-lined pattern. In other words: the trees are generated by taking a micro-pattern and replicating it onto itself over and over (somewhat like a recursive fractal). Our next diagram (Figure 3) shows the two micro-patterns, their reiterations, and then the final trees (which are actually the result of four further reiterations).

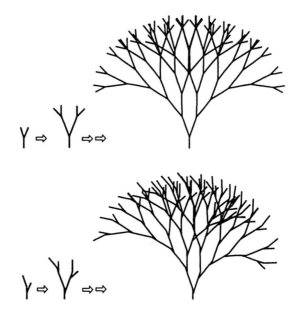

FIGURE 3. Reiterative
Components of Trees

Notice that although the two trees are quite different in many ways, the recursive patterns generating them are quite close: the first tree is constructed out of a "Y" shape and the second varies only in that the right branch of the "Y" is lower on the trunk than the left branch.

Those who have studied other cultures or subcultures often have a similar experience. At first the other culture may not seem so radically different from what is familiar. There may be families, for example, some form of economic or bartering exchange, some mode of housing, some hierarchy of class or leadership, roles defined by gender or age, and so forth. Like the two trees, the new culture may seem a different member of the same species. As one enters the culture more intimately, however, a profound sense of difference may emerge. Comparisons become more hazardous and may even seem impossible, as awkward as the comparison in Figure 2. Finally, as one enters the culture still more deeply, it begins to make sense in its own terms. Once one penetrates an aspect of the culture profoundly, it seems the other aspects are assimilated more easily. One may even be able to predict behavior one has not seen before. It is as if one suddenly found oneself in a new part of the tree but already knew where the next branch would split off. This indicates the discovery of cultural recursivity: a repetitive pattern out of which the whole is constructed. The person may then find that new experiences in the culture are familiar in some way—not necessarily because they repeat patterns from one's own home culture (the kind of similarities first felt when entering the new culture) but because they are reminiscent of patterns previously experienced in the new culture.

If cultures are indeed recursive in the way just suggested, it is possible to compare them in a more or less holistic way—at least in one important sense. We have seen that we can talk pointedly about both the similarities and differences between the two trees by noting their respective recursive elements and their cumulative reiterative effects. If we can isolate a reiterative factor in different kinds of cultures, perhaps we can also talk holistically about their similarities and differences. That is the project of this book. The recursive cultural patterns I will call the orientations of "intimacy" and "integrity." Our study will focus on how we can generate a very different cultural understanding of fact and value, of what-is and what-should-be, by reiterating this pattern over and over again into ever more complex theoretical manifestations.

This book is not a study of any particular culture, although I cannot deny I have often had specific cultures or subcultures in mind as I developed the theory. As the next chapter will explain, for example, I doubt that I would have developed the reiterative patterns in this way if it had not been for my exposure to Japanese culture. Yet the book is not intended to be an analysis of any single culture, even Japanese culture. It is more like a thought experiment that raises fundamental issues about the nature of culture itself, especially the relation between culture and thought. One aim of this book is to present the case for understanding at least some cultural phenomena in terms of the reiterative or recursive analysis. The role of the philosopher is not just to analyze but also to give us better tools for analysis. My readers are therefore invited, indeed encouraged, to use the tools in relation to whatever cultures or subcultures they wish. It is unlikely that any culture is ever a perfect example of either an intimacy-dominant or integrity-dominant culture (generalities always have qualifications or exceptions), but the hope is that the analysis and critical tools presented here may help us see connections and differences we might have otherwise missed. If this hope is realized, communication and understanding across cultures will be assisted and the book will have served its ultimate purpose.

# CHAPTER I

# CULTURAL ORIENTATIONS

One of the most basic questions we can ask is how things are related. Relationship is fundamental to philosophy insofar as philosophy concerns itself with key relations: self and world, self and other, knower and known, thing and thing, and so forth. This book explores two essentially different ways of relating. As we saw with the two situations in the Introduction, a person can construct quite different orientations in understanding the world and acting within it. As our inquiry progresses, we will witness the unfolding of two different worldviews, two different ways of understanding the self, and two different ways of constructing value.

In explaining this issue I have come to think of it as a problem in "cultural philosophy." I choose this term because it suggests two different meanings. First, cultural philosophy can mean a philosophy of culture. That is: it may be useful to bring philosophical analysis to our understanding of culture just as we bring it to our analyses of art, politics, ethics, knowledge, or gender. Philosophers may study culture as part of a larger concern for understanding human existence—its possibilities and its limitations. A philosophy of culture may be able to tell us something about how to understand the individual and social dimensions of human being as well as suggest how it might best be lived. In its ability to be prescriptive as well as descriptive, moreover, philosophy might take us into areas of cultural understanding outside the domains of sociology or anthropology as we usually construe them. This book suggests that cultures or subcultures often emphasize one form of relationship over the other. And this has profound consequences for how people in the culture tend to think, explain, value, and persuade. In philosophically analyzing the two orientations of intimacy and integrity, we will gain insight into how and why cultures differ.

A second meaning of cultural philosophy is that philosophy itself is a cultural enterprise in certain fundamental respects. Philosophers sometimes think of their discipline as searching for eternal, transcultural truths, but perhaps this very tendency is related to cultural conditions. Philosophy does not arise in vacuo. It necessarily draws on a cultural legacy for its terminology, conceptualization of problems, and even relevance. Philosophy develops not in total isolation but within a community of discourse. It is hard to imagine that today's Western philosophers would be as interested in cognitive science, for example, were it not for the impact of computers on our society. Similarly, mind/body issues assume a new pertinence in an age of neuroscience, neurosurgery, psychotropic drugs, and a regimen for "harvesting" human organs that depends on defining death in terms of the lack of brain function. If all of this is obvious enough, why is it so common for philosophers, especially Western philosophers, to think of their work as having transcultural, universal significance? Perhaps at least some of the answer lies in the cultural history of Western philosophy itself.

A key point in this cultural history was the emergence of Western philosophy in the city-state of Athens during the fourth century B.C.E. The Athenians had developed one of the many civilizations surrounding the Mediterranean in that era. Significantly Plato and Aristotle, patriarchs of the Western philosophical tradition, developed their philosophies in Athens at the very time Athenian culture was most imperiled. Athens had lost the Peloponnesian War to Sparta, and Macedonia was already extending its power into the Peloponnesus. And there was still the threat from the East, as the wars with Persia had shown. In short, Western philosophy took root in Athens during an era of military and cultural infringement. At the same time, there was even in peacetime a need for cross-cultural understanding and exchange. For purposes of trade, if nothing else, it was important for Mediterranean peoples to recognize their common interests as well as their differences. This sense of cultural pluralism within a larger Mediterranean identity intensified with the subsequent expansion of the Alexandrine and Roman empires and then again with the spread of

Christianity and Islam. In such a context it was understandable that the Athenian philosophers of the fourth century B.C.E. would seek an understanding of self, world, and value that would be equally valid whether one lived under the military and cultural sphere of the Spartans, the Persians, or the Macedonians. Just as Greek became the lingua franca of the whole region, Greek philosophy set out to become a universal currency of intellectual exchange.

A narrative of the history of Western philosophy, therefore, could easily start with this quest for a universal, cross-cultural, or pancultural ground to thought and value. The quest would begin with Plato's Forms and continue through Aristotle's fourfold causality, the medieval and scholastic notion of God, the Renaissance and Enlightenment's universal application of mathematics, and the twentieth century's emphasis on formal logic. In these contexts philosophy developed as a means of bridging contexts, cultures, time, and place. Such an understanding of philosophy became dominant in the West.

Philosophy can serve a different purpose, however. It has often been a means of differentiating one group from another, for example, giving that group acknowledgment or recognition from outsiders as well as an internal identity. In this manifestation, philosophy might be said to be "for a people" instead of "for the world." Esoteric traditions, East and West, often understood philosophy in this way: philosophy was developed for a select group and used as one of its defining characteristics. The Gnostics and the mystery cults of the ancient world were often secret societies whose definition centered on an esoteric knowledge. Religious philosophies—including at some points those found in Christianity, Islam, Judaism, and Shinto—could function in a similar way.

Even in our own times we sometimes find philosophies primarily aimed at analyzing or defining "us"—where "us" might mean a particular group instead of all humanity at all times in all places. Examples include some (but, of course, not all) forms of "philosophies of the oppressed," where the "us" could mean, for example, the proletariat, people of color, the subaltern, women, the colonized, and so forth. The universalizing paradigm dominant in much of Western philosophy has often struggled to exclude such self-avowedly cultural, social, and historical philosophies, claiming that they are not philosophies at all. The irony of course (an irony that these excluded philosophies inevitably point out) is that in insisting that philosophy be "universal," the dominant Western tradition inadvertently shows its own social, historical, and cultural roots. The insistence on universalization boils down to one cultural philosophy's trying to exclude the very possibility of another.

The self-acclaimed cultural philosophies can slip into a different error, however—that of trying to maintain relativity in an absolute way. In rejecting the dominant mode of Western philosophy, there is a danger of throwing out the baby with the bath water. In fact, it is not a case of a single baby but twins. One twin is discarded when someone asserts that there is *nothing* universal or pancultural. The flaw in such a claim (one that the universalist philosophers inevitably point out) is that the statement is itself universal: to make a claim about either nothing or everything is logically a statement in universal form. Unperturbed, the radical relativist may then make the error of throwing out the other twin. Often this takes the form of rejecting all logic itself as "patriarchal," "Western," "racist," or "hegemonic." This is a fatal error for two reasons: first, it cuts off the possibility of discourse within as well as outside the cultural group; second, it misidentifies the problem and therefore lets the real danger go unchecked. Let us briefly consider each aspect.

First "logic"—if we include in this term even the most fundamental or formal rules of reasoning such as the law of noncontradiction—is important to the conception of every kind of critical or philosophical discourse. This is true regardless of whether the philosophy is self-described as either cultural or universal. Why? Because such a basic law of logic is not about truth but intelligibility. As Aristotle noted when he first articulated the law of noncontradiction: to contradict oneself is not to speak a falsehood, but to say nothing at all. If someone asserts both $p$ and not-$p$, this means that both $p$ and not-$p$ are supposed to be true in exactly the same way at exactly the same time. Such an assertion is unintelligible; it has no meaning that can be judged true or false. One can neither agree nor disagree with it. (Agreement and disagreement assume that what is false at one time and in one way cannot be true at the same time and in the same way—and vice versa.) To deny the law of noncontradiction would make discussion and critical thinking impossible not only between cultures but within any culture.

Second, the radical relativist is justifiably suspicious about something here. But the problem is not the formal logic itself. Instead the problem is the *misapplication* of this logic to justify a particular worldview. Logic can tell us how to think and express ourselves clearly, but it can tell us absolutely nothing whatsoever about either the way the world is or the way it should be. No worldview follows from intelligibility. Intelligibility and its formalization as fundamental rules of logic can only help us articulate a particular worldview—a worldview that may or may not be accurate. Logic requires only that we, not reality, make sense. If an individual or a group misconstrues this relationship and tries to go directly from logic to ontology, only then do we find the situation that someone might want to label "patriarchal," "hegemonic," "Western," or whatever. Logic is a tool used to sharpen analysis, thinking, or articulation—not a weapon to bludgeon to death any philosophical position one does not like. The point is to describe the way things are with as much logical clarity as possible; the error is to use logical clarity as the main criterion for the way things are.

To sum up: from these two meanings of cultural philosophy (the philosophy of culture and philosophy as culturally embedded), we can say that philosophy and culture are in a symbiotic, dialectical, or mutually influential relation. Although a philosophy is itself a cultural phenomenon, it can not only understand but also change a culture. Meanwhile, a culture reflects or assumes a philosophy or set of affiliated philosophies even as it influences the framework within which philosophy takes shape.

It is important to remember throughout the ensuing analysis, as noted in the Introduction, that a society is seldom culturally monolithic. Alternatively, one could say that within a culture are various subcultures which may not be in complete harmony with each other. Still, in every society there seems to be a dominant culture that claims the mantle of "authority," "tradition," and "the educated." It establishes the "mainstream" system of thought and value with which the subcultures (or the subaltern or marginalized philosophies) may well disagree, at least in part. Therefore, in talking about cultural differences I could just as readily talk about differences among subcultures within a single society. The importance of this point will become more evident as our analysis proceeds.

Although there are exceptions, Western philosophers have not commonly developed cultural philosophies. Hence the reader might wonder how I came upon this topic. A philosophical position is an answer to a specific question, and no question is without context, including personal context. What circumstances contributed to my interests and my questions? Although much of my formal training was in Western philosophy, for the last quarter century I have also been a student of Japanese philosophy. When I began studying Asian philosophy as a graduate student, I suppose I had hoped that my research into these traditions might shed light on the problems in the Western tradition to which I had become so accustomed. How did Asian thinkers traditionally deal with the problems of, say, freedom and determinism, mind/body dualism, or the relation between universals and particulars? As I progressed in my study, however, I realized that the Asian traditions, especially the East Asian traditions of China and Japan, did not have prepackaged answers to the great philosophical issues of the West. It was not so much that the Chinese and Japanese thinkers had different answers to the same questions Western thinkers had asked. They seemed to be asking quite different questions.

In studying Japanese philosophy, therefore, for me the issue gradually shifted from looking for answers to my Western questions to looking more closely at the questions the Japanese themselves had asked. Where did their questions come from? What made them different from most of the West's philosophical questions? I was not, of course, the first Western-er to notice that Japanese culture was different from the West in this respect. But unlike many of my predecessors, I found it misleading to talk about Japanese thinking as if it differed logically (in the formal sense explained above) from the West's. Much of the early literature in comparative philosophy, for example, depicted the Japanese as "aesthetic" rather than "theoretic" or "rationalistic," as "ante-scientific" rather than "scientific," as "concrete" or "phenomenalistic" rather than "abstract." The scholars who made these characterizations were not fools; they were onto something very significant. Yet I found the way they formulated their depictions to be misleading. It seemed to suggest—and sometimes even explicitly stated—that the Japanese either do not think logically or do not think very much at all.

The circumstances in which I began my study of Japan in 1972 un-doubtedly influenced my skepticism toward such descriptions. Although the earlier characterizations of Japan might have worked well enough for discussions of bonsai, haiku, or ink-wash paintings, how could they be seen as anything but caricatures in the ascendant era of Honda, Sony, Nikon, and Epson? The (perhaps orientalist) characterizations could not explain how the Japanese could excel at enterprises that seemed to re-quire theoretical, abstract, and logical thought. Starting with the insights of my predecessors, I investigated the issue of how Japanese think about things. Formally trained as a philosopher, I was delighted to discover that there was a modern academic tradition in Japan that called itself "philos-ophy" *(tetsugaku,* "sagacity" + "-ology," the term the Japanese invented in the late nineteenth century to translate the Western word). Some Japanese philosophers limited themselves to the study of Western philosophy, but others developed philosophies of their own. The most noted members of this group belonged to the "Kyoto school," which included such creative thinkers as NISHIDA Kitarō, TANABE Hajime, MIKI Kiyoshi, and NISHITANI Keiji. At the time only a few of their writings were available in Western languages, so I had to learn Japanese to do any philosophical explorations on my own.

I discovered that many of these philosophers were conversant with both traditional and contemporary Western philosophy (especially from the European continent), as well as Asian traditions from the mainland. What especially intrigued me, however, was that many modern Japanese philosophers had a particular interest in Zen Buddhism. According to what I had read in English, Zen was an irrational (or nonrational) tradition with a distaste for anything philosophical. I thought that if I studied Zen (both the practice and the writings), I might get a clue to the connective, invisible mycelium that mushroomed into such seemingly disconnected phenomena as Bashō's haiku and Morita's Sony Corporation. To determine whether the Japanese actually think differently from Westerners, it seemed a good idea to look at the paradigmatic case of what seemed least like Western rationality—namely, Zen Buddhism. That is: I tried to make sense of Japanese culture by starting with what the West found most nonsensical.

In my study, however, I discovered that Zen did indeed make sense and I could understand why it might be influential on modern academic philosophy in Japan. Even when I examined the common Zen Buddhist statements that seem to be in the form of "*a* is not-*a*," I found on closer examination that the way something was "*a*" was not at the same time and in the same way as it was "not-*a*." In other words: although certain Japanese forms of Buddhist rhetoric might be especially fond of paradoxes, there was not necessarily any violation of Aristotle's law of non-contradiction. The paradox was to be resolved by some deeper insight; the paradox was only an *apparent* contradiction, a provocative starting point to lead one to a new standpoint from which what had formally seemed logically incompatible was now no longer so. Although the practical route to the new standpoint was not via logical analysis, I found nothing illogical in the standpoint itself.

The result of my research appeared in 1981 in a book called *Zen Action/Zen Person*. Just before publication, I sent a copy of the manuscript to two colleagues for their response. One was an American philosopher with a deep personal interest in Zen who had read virtually everything on Zen available in Western languages. The other was a specialist on Japanese thought, a Japanese who could read English comfortably. The responses were interesting: the American liked the book very much, noting that it was "totally unlike any other book on Zen in English." The Japanese colleague was favorably impressed, too, although he confided to a colleague in Japan that he was a bit surprised that my analysis "had remained so close to the traditional interpretation of Zen." These reactions suggested that the nature of Japanese thought was not being adequately described to Westerners. Here was a problem of cultural difference requiring further study.

What exactly do we mean by a "cultural difference"? If the difference does not stem from the fundamental forms of thinking, whence does it come? The real disparity lies, I believe, in what aspect of our humanness a cultural tradition tends to emphasize, enhance, and preserve as central. What is foreground in one culture may be background in another. Therefore, it is not so much that the Japanese think differently from Westerners. Rather, to put it simply, they tend to think about different things—to pick out different aspects of a phenomenon as the part most worthy of attention. Of course, if cultures focus on different aspects of phenomena they become increasingly adept and sophisticated at analyzing "what is important," that is, what is important to *them*. They develop technical vocabulary, distinctive arguments, and sets of questions deriving from the answers to former questions. A philosophical tradition is then under way and it develops in symbiotic relation to its culture's values. In short: culture shapes the way we experience the world of meanings, and the world of meanings developed through intellectual reflection ("philosophy") becomes the stuff of cultural tradition. Because this idea of cultures giving us gestalts on reality is going to be a useful model at various points in this book, it is worthwhile to pause here to analyze the idea a bit further.

Let us consider four visual examples (Figures 4–7). Figure 4 is a picture often used to explain the difference between figure and ground in gestalt psychology. Whether you see it as a picture of a black goblet or as two facial silhouettes in white depends on your take. What is the focal point of the picture and what is the background? In this example, once you know the picture can be given meaning in two ways, it is rather easy to go back and forth between the two gestalts. You can see the two possibilities without privileging one over the other.

Most people find the shift between gestalts in Figure 5 to be rather

FIGURE 4. Goblet or Faces?

FIGURE 5. Old Woman or Young Woman?

harder. Is Figure 5 an old woman with her head tilted down and cheek buried in her coat? Or is it a young woman looking over her right shoulder? Unlike the first example, with Figure 5 most people see one gestalt more readily than the other and have to work to see an alternative. Even when both gestalts can be seen, many people still seem to favor one or the other when they first look back at the picture. Now let us turn to two further examples a little more abstract.

Most people immediately see Figure 6 as the representation of a transparent cube, but Figure 7 not quite so readily. When we think about it, however, we realize that Figure 7 is as accurate a two-dimensional portrayal of a cube as Figure 6—but Figure 6 is the way we have generally been taught to represent a cube. Because of this training, one image seems a more "natural" way of representing a cube than the other.

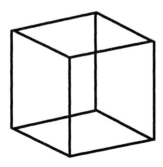

FIGURE 6. "Standard" Cube

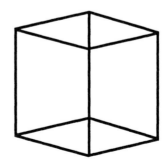

FIGURE 7. "Nonstandard" Cube

Obviously, in saying "natural" we do not mean there is an innate preference for one over the other. Rather, it is "second nature," a culturally ingrained preference.

In interpreting these gestalt images, the first question to investigate
is this: how was it possible to see the pictures in different ways? What did
we have to do in order to shift from one gestalt to another? It seems
the shift did not involve analysis so much as *imagination*. Through the
imagination we could reverse foreground or background and thereby
construct different meaning out of what was there. The question I then
explored in my study of comparative culture was whether it is possible
to do something similar with the more complex gestalt processes of different cultures. Is it possible for a person who has been raised and educated in English-speaking North America to imagine a different cultural
worldview—specifically a Japanese way of experiencing the world? I do
not necessarily mean we would actually be able to *experience* the world in
the same way as a Japanese. This would be possible only after decades of
exposure and study. But could we *imagine* what it would be like? Could
we shift our foregrounding and gestalt processes as a kind of thought experiment, getting a glimpse at least of how the apparently same thing
could be seen differently? Over the years I experimented with different
techniques for giving Western audiences a glimpse into how things could
be interpreted differently—how one might get a feel for a Japanese view
of the world. The trick was to find a way of switching periphery and center, background and foreground, ground and figure, in the audience's
firmly embedded cultural gestalts.

Eventually I came upon a technique to do this simply and quickly if
only fleetingly. The technique is based on a simple assumption. I presup-
posed that what Westerners needed in order to imagine themselves into a
Japanese worldview was already there in their own experience—but on
the *periphery* of what they normally made the focal point for analysis and
value. That is: there are kinds of phenomena everyone has experienced.
In one culture, these experiences may be considered the most interesting
for analysis, the most revealing of our basic humanity, the most fruitful to
emphasize. In another culture, however, they might be considered common, not particularly revealing of anything central or important, and in
short not worth thinking about very much. If we could then reverse the
preference and focus on what is not normally emphasized in our culture,
we might be able to attain quite suddenly a glimpse into the other culture. The thrust of this "cultural insight training," as I call it, is not to

give the audience more information about the other culture. Instead the idea is to urge the audience to get a different take on phenomena already available to them. In using this technique to explain Japanese culture, I suggested that my audience use their imaginations to conjure up ordinary experiences laden with a sense of what I called "intimacy." Frequently I used the following six vignettes.

Image I: Think of what it is like to be with your spouse or a lifelong dear friend. Such a person is someone to whom you feel you can say anything, but you need say nothing in order to be understood. A little pucker of the lip, a twitch in the eye, a movement of the eyebrow, a barely audible sigh says it all.

Image II: Someone steals your wallet. Both the money and the treasured family pictures—negatives lost long ago—are gone. The money belonged to you; it was your money. But the pictures belonged *with* you not to you. In taking the photos, the thief stole part of your self, not merely something external like the money over which you held temporary title.

Image III: You see your daughter after she comes home from school. You know something is wrong. You can't put your finger on it, and you can't explain how you know, but you do know she will pick at her dinner and look at television tonight without really watching it. You even know when you ask her what's wrong, she'll say "nothing's wrong."

Image IV: You've been working on a piano piece for months, endlessly drilling the progressions and chords, getting the technique down perfectly. One day, quite unexpectedly, the awareness of technique disappears. You are playing the same notes as always, but today it is completely different. You feel you are not playing the music; rather, the music is playing through you.

Image V: Michelangelo looks at the discarded block of marble given to him. He wonders what to do with it. Studying the marble, the image of David appears within it and the artist sets to work releasing David from his stone case.

Image VI: After traveling for some weeks, you return home. You take a little stroll around the yard, go into the house, sit in your favorite chair, and a close friend drops by to ask about your trip. You feel yourself relax as you let down your defenses and give yourself up to the familiar. You feel you are really home.

These experiences are not in any way particularly Japanese. We all have experiences of this nature regardless of our cultural context. Yet in cultures that place an emphasis on intimacy, such experiences are foregrounded as being important and worthy of analysis. Technical terms are developed to express nuances about them; they become paradigmatic cases for understanding what is most central in acts of relating, whether to other people or other things. In Latin, *"intimus"* means either "what is innermost" or "a close friend." The verb *"intimāre"* means "to make known." Putting this together, we can say that the root meaning of intimacy is something like "making known to a close friend what is innermost." Thus intimacy involves an inseparability, a belonging together, a sharing. We have many friends and advisers, but only a few *intimates.* Many things are in relation, but only some are *intimately* related. We know many things, but have *intimate* knowledge of only a few. We express many things, but only those in our inner circle understand what we *intimate.*

In the next chapter I will analyze intimacy in detail. But for now we can list five fundamental characteristics:

1.  Intimacy is objective, but personal rather than public.
2.  In an intimate relation, self and other belong together in a way that does not sharply distinguish the two.
3.  Intimate knowledge has an affective dimension.
4.  Intimacy is somatic as well as psychological.
5.  Intimacy's ground is not generally self-conscious, reflective, or self-illuminating.

When I used the concept of intimacy as a heuristic for understanding central orientations in Japanese culture, I frequently made contrasts with the dominant culture of the modern West—that is, the culture of Western philosophical modernism starting with Descartes and culminating in eighteenth- and nineteenth-century movements like the Enlightenment and positivism. In doing so, I would often be asked the following question: if Japanese culture (with many important exceptions, of course) can be characterized as highlighting a fundamental orientation toward, and emphasis on, intimacy, how might we characterize contemporary American culture? I gave this modern Western orientation the name "integrity."

Integrity is that which emphasizes the following (in almost direct opposition to the emphases of intimacy):

1. Objectivity as public verifiability
2. External over internal relations
3. Knowledge as ideally empty of affect
4. The intellectual and psychological as distinct from the somatic
5. Knowledge as reflective and self-conscious of its own grounds

In chapter 3 we will examine these characteristics in detail. Why is "integrity" an appropriate term? Again we may start with the historical roots
of the word. The Latin *"integritās"* is related to *"integer,"* meaning an
indivisible whole. We call whole numbers "integers" because they are not
fractionalized. The Latin *"integer"* in turn is probably related to *"in"* +
*"tegere"* or *"in"* + *"tangere,"* that is, "not" + "touch." That which has integrity is untouched, uncorrupted, pure. A person of integrity will not
sell out. The integrity of a ship's hull will keep it afloat. In short, the etymological meaning of integrity suggests "being whole, indivisible, and
inviolable."

In comparing the Japanese and American cultures, therefore, I frequently characterized them as cultures in which intimacy and integrity
were respectively emphasized. These are heuristic generalizations—a gestalt allowing one to focus on what each culture tends to consider central, authoritative, or mainstream. In this light, the heuristic also makes
the exceptions stand out more sharply. In developing these heuristic categories I further refined the analysis of both orientations. And to my initial surprise, audiences and readers found the comparison applicable to
other cultures with which they were familiar. Furthermore, the idea of
cultures sometimes expanded to issues such as the construction of gender. Many commented that it seemed, at least in Western European cultures, that the feminine gender was traditionally constructed in ways to
emphasize intimacy while the masculine emphasized integrity. Others saw
the rise of philosophical modernity in the West as a transition from a
medieval emphasis on intimacy to one based primarily on integrity. Still
others thought of subcultures within the United States that seemed to be
oriented more toward intimacy than integrity. Might it not be useful to
generalize these two orientations even further by making no reference to

specific cultures (except insofar as a concrete example here or there might be helpful)? Just how widely can the distinction be applied? Given my original interests in cultural philosophy, I became especially interested in learning what worldviews might be generated from each orientation and, consequently, what philosophical questions might arise. In the next two chapters, therefore, we turn to the general explication of intimacy and integrity.

# CHAPTER 2

# WHAT IS INTIMACY?

In this chapter we will develop our analysis of intimacy as an orientation emphasizing certain modes of relationship. Our inquiry will take us on an exploratory journey into our own experience, pointing out a cluster of phenomena and values probably familiar to all of us but not typically given much emphasis in cultures with a strong integrity orientation. For readers from such integrity-dominant cultures (as perhaps most readers of a book in English today are likely to be), this chapter may delineate another profile of themselves as human beings. It is as if Figure 5, the gestalt picture in chapter 1, were not of two different women but of two different images of the same person, both real, but only one of which has been given much philosophical attention up to now.

What can we say about intimacy in human life? When people hear the word "intimacy," they may first think of lingerie, French perfume, and sex manuals. To develop any insight into this important dimension of ourselves, however, it is necessary to resist any reduction of intimacy to mere sexual intimacy. We do use the word, after all, in a variety of other ways. We commonly speak, for example, of someone's intimate knowledge of tax laws, or of someone's being intimate to a secret, or even of the intimate relation between inflation and unemployment. In fact, the word might seem to assume so many diverse senses that it lacks any core meaning at all. It is possible, however, to sift out a set of characteristics, or at least a set of family resemblances, in the various uses of the term, entitling us to use the word in its multiple contexts. That is the project of this chapter: to dig into the concept and its associated phenomena until we unearth its deeper structure.

As noted in chapter 1, the Latin etymology of the term conjures up the following image: intimacy is making known *(intimāre)* to a close friend *(intimus* or *intima)* what is innermost *(intimus)*. In other words: intimacy is most essentially a sharing of innermost qualities. In nonhuman relations, the inseparability derives from the inherent qualities of the things themselves. We speak of the intimate relation between flora and fauna in a particular ecosystem, for example, or between matter and energy in the context of particle physics. In such cases, we cannot fully understand one side of the pair without considering the other. Although we can conceptually isolate the two through abstraction, they are really intertwined: we cannot divorce what one is by nature from what the other is by nature.

In thinking of intimacy, people usually have in mind intimacy among persons, not things. Here is a significant difference in the way intimacy works. Among nonhuman things, intimacy derives from how things are and must be; but among humans, intimacy is achieved. Interpersonal intimacy requires opening up the innermost—one's thoughts, feelings, and motives—in order to share them with the other. There is intimacy between lovers, between parent and child, between master and apprentice, between friends. When I know someone intimately, I know what makes that person tick. I know the person from the inside, sharing that person's psychological space. When my desire for a closer relationship is denied, I feel shut out: the other person will not let me in. When the other person does reciprocate, however, we may eventually achieve a level of accord wherein each of us is immediately aware of the other's inner dynamics.

In an intimate context people feel free to say anything, to share their inner secrets. Trust permeates the conversation. This interchange may be an utterly free flow of conversation because the conversants already know each other intimately and there is no need (indeed no possibility) of censuring or hiding what is innermost. Paradoxically, along with this free flow of conversation, the more profound the interpersonal intimacy, the more that can be left unsaid. The need to be explicit, the effort to explain, the urge to fill in the silence—all become muted in ever deepening levels of intimation where the slightest gesture or facial expression may express more than enough.

Moreover, intimates do not have to think about each other explicitly in discursive or step-by-step analyses. As noted in one of the vignettes from chapter 1, a parent may deeply understand the child without being able to specify exactly how this understanding comes about. The intimate knowledge of another person is based not on detached observation and logic, but on years of sharing and caring. Intimate knowledge of the other person comes from empathy, what the Germans call *Einfühlung*, literally an entrance into the other person's feelings.

Insofar as intimacy among human beings involves choice, the intimate bond depends on both parties' continued consent and commitment. Unlike the intimate connections between things such as matter and energy or flora and fauna, human intimacy can always be broken: by death, by circumstance, by choice. The shattering of intimacy can contribute to the agony of a divorce, for example. The time and effort invested in the relationship were originally rewarded with the positive benefits of intimation: the most efficient, direct, and effortless form of human communication. Whenever the trust grounding intimacy erodes, however, the intimations can become vicious and stinging. Physical proximity becomes painful as each utterance, each gesture, each act suggests the underlying hostility in the alienated couple. The tension in a degenerating relationship is devastating, not because communication has broken down, but because it continues to be so good that cruelty functions at an unbearable level. As the idiom says, the two people "know how to push each other's buttons." Only when the formal bonds are completely severed, however, can the former intimates begin to fathom their loss. It will take years for them to form new relationships enjoying the previous levels of intimacy. In the interim, they must constantly go through the effort of having to explain themselves to nonintimates while puzzling through what their new partners might really mean.

Thus far we have considered the intimacy between two things and the intimacy between two people. What about the intimacy between a person and a nonperson? An intimate diary, for example, contains private details about oneself ordinarily shared only with intimates. An intimate café is one whose coziness lends itself to private, personal conversation. We might say a diary is an intimacy with oneself, the diary assuming the status of an imagined intimate, sometimes even personified in phrases like "Dear Diary." The café, by contrast, is not itself intimate but a locus supporting intimacy among its patrons. Yet not all forms of intimacy between persons and nonpersons are construed in these two ways. Consider how a chess master has an intimate grasp of chess openings, or a mathematician of non-Euclidean geometries, or a historian of medieval military history. What makes the knowledge of a theory or field intimate? Yes, the person must command the material: intimate knowledge is always extensive. Just as important, however, it is also intensive: the person displays a personal involvement with, even a fondness or ardor for, the ideas. The subject matter is not merely what the person understands; it is also part of what the person is. In other words: when a person knows a subject intimately, it becomes part of that person's way of perceiving and acting in the world. In maneuvering to get a seat on a crowded train, the chess master may see her own actions as a gambit, the mathematician as a topological problem, the military historian as a campaign. Precisely because they see the world through their consuming interests, everyday activities deepen their insight into their specialty. In short: in the intimate knowledge of concepts, the intimacy is imparted by one's personal involvement with the subject.

Similar characteristics apply to intimately knowing a physical, rather than conceptual, object. Sculptors know their chisels intimately; cabinet-makers know their planes. When a master artist is at work, the tools seem to function as expressions of the hands. When a person knows a tool's use intimately, technique becomes second nature—that is, it becomes part of the person's own nature, part of her or his personal style. To an art historian, the artist's brushwork is as distinctive as a fingerprint. Indeed, the brushwork is ultimately a gesture, a physical intimation of the artist's inner self.

This brings us back to the issue of openness. As we have seen, in the case of intimate relationships among nonhuman entities the intimacy is a given; it derives from the character of the things themselves. In interpersonal relationships, by contrast, both persons must open themselves to intimacy; intimacy for them is an achievement. What, then, can we say about the human/nonhuman relationship? How does a person open oneself to an intimate relationship with a thing? Let us analyze an example:

> My neighbor smiled broadly as he watched me split firewood for the first time. The job was getting done, but it was taking its toll on my body. My arms were exhausted after splitting just a few logs. Each blow was a great effort, ending in a shock as I smashed the ax through the wood into the stump. Finally, I looked at my friend with chagrin, "I'm not doing it right, am I?" He replied, "Let the ax do the work, not your shoulders." He then gave me some tips on stance, on reading the checks in the

wood, and on executing the swing. The most important lesson was that I had to rear back and just start the ax on its way, letting the axhead slice right through the log. My arms and shoulders no longer pushed the ax through its flight; they just gave it an initial impetus and guided its arc. In effect, I had to relinquish my self-conscious attempt to slash the wood; I had to learn to yield to the design of the ax and the character of the log.

Even this primitive relationship between a person and a thing exemplifies the need for one to be open to the nature of the tool and its object, allowing them to become intimately connected with one's intention. Just as I move my fingers across a typewriter without any self-conscious effort, I had to let the ax become, as it were, an extension of my body without any intruding concepts or emotions. Like all impersonal entities, the ax, just by being the ax, was ready for me to know it intimately in my log splitting. I, on the contrary, had to let myself accept the ax's character. I had to fathom and appreciate its inner structure—its long handle, the weight and design of its head, and so on—so that its essential character could merge with my inner intent. I also had to be open to the log's internal structure: where it would allow, and where it would resist, being split. In short: whether relating to another person or to a thing, a human being must choose to make oneself available to intimate relations. We humans are not innately intimate: intimacy is an accomplishment.

Because human beings must choose whether to engage in intimacy, we prefer to choose with whom we form an intimate relationship. We resent any coercion. A waitress is entitled to feel insulted when a male customer calls her "honey." The term implies an intimacy that is not there and, at least on the woman's part, not desired. In fact, to deny a person the privilege to choose one's intimates is to deny that person's humanity. Such sexism, racism, or classism, for example, reifies the person in the sense that it treats a human being like a thing inherently self-disclosed and accessible to any human who wants to be in some kind of intimate relation with it. By saying she is not a sex object, the waitress affirms she is not a sexual tool, a thing by nature open to the man's intimate use.

Precisely because they risk privacy, intimate relations can also, paradoxically, be a means of preserving privacy. In times of anguish, for instance, I may desperately need another person's comfort, but it is hard to express my feelings nakedly, publicly, and in detail. We refer to the anxiety and embarrassment of "baring one's soul" to another person. How consoling it is to have someone who already knows me so intimately that I do not have to say anything to be explicitly understood. Through my intimates, I share my inner life without having to disclose it publicly. Intimate communication ("intimation") is, in fact, an encoded expressiveness. It opens a person in such a way that only intimates can decipher the message. A person's innermost world, like all secrets, aches to be expressed, but it might be too revealing, too risky, to do so in a public manner. Once made public, a person's inner self may be unscrupulously used by others as objects for their own benefit or amusement. The desire to share, therefore, is outweighed only by the fear of being violated. Through intimations to those they trust, however, people can reap the benefits of self-disclosure while minimizing the risk of vulnerability: we share our inner life while maintaining some degree of privacy with respect to those outside the intimate circle, those who do not know how to read the intimations.

Now oriented to some of the experiences and ideas relevant to studying intimacy, let us examine its characteristics in a more systematic manner. In discussing such relations we have already, directly or indirectly, referred to the following:

1.  Intimacy is objective, but personal rather than public.
2.  In an intimate relation, the self and other belong together in a way that does not sharply distinguish the two.
3.  Intimate knowledge has an affective dimension.
4.  Intimacy is somatic as well as psychological.
5.  The ground of intimacy is not generally self-conscious, reflective, or self-illuminating.

Let us consider each of these central features separately.

## INTIMACY AS PERSONAL

We have already noted that intimacy makes known the innermost self. Through the indirect suggestiveness of intimation, people express themselves to another without exposure to everyone. This implies that a person within an intimate locus learns in a manner quite different from one who acquires publicly available information. Most forms of knowledge are public insofar as their grounds are accessible to any interested party or at least anyone with the appropriate equipment. In claiming to know something, I can generally support my assertion by giving evidence that others can investigate for themselves. If I say, for example, that it is now three o'clock, I can give my reasons for saying so: both my watch and the clock on the wall back up my claim. A skeptic could check those sources and others like it (calling a time-of-day service on the telephone, for instance) to verify the reliability of my statement. This stress on public verification is a sign of modernity. The dominant modern Western orientation tends to understand truth as something that anyone can certify through her or his own experience, rather than, say, what a particular book or specially designated person might assert. The hallucinatory accusation by some person in authority is no longer an acceptable reason for burning someone at the stake as a witch. The modern West, at least ideally, has made the commonality of human experience its authority and public verifiability its method. This kind of modernism has tried to replace ignorance, superstition, and inquisition with reason, observation, and justice.

Still, we should not go so far as to reject outright all other varieties of knowing. I know, for instance, what I am now thinking and, usually, what I am now feeling (even though there may be cases in which it is difficult to explain myself adequately). It would be foolish, even insane, to deny this simple fact. Yet no known instrument can verify this inner awareness. I cannot project the image of a cross-section of my thoughts and publicly demonstrate that indeed I was thinking about how much I would like a hot fudge sundae. If you ask me to prove empirically what I was thinking about, I cannot. Despite the lack of public verification, however, I am still justifiably confident I know what I am thinking as I think it. Indeed, as any Cartesian would point out, even if I doubted that belief I would still know I was doubting it. Thus we know a great deal about our inner states. And although this knowledge is generally not publicly verifiable, it still deserves to be considered knowledge insofar as it is a legitimate basis for making claims about certain aspects of reality.

Proceeding to a more intricate example, consider the everyday situation in which two people are said to know each other's thoughts. Spouses are often so intimately linked that each knows what the other is thinking without having to utter a word. Even without resorting to telepathy, the couple can learn to read subtle external signs suggestive of inner phenomena. This is hardly public verification in any empirical sense. My wife may know exactly what feeling or thought accompanies my facial expression. But to someone outside my intimate circle, the same expression may be as puzzling as a map without a legend. Such an expression is communication through intimation, the encoded language which allows an intimate into my private domain without making that realm public.

The theories of knowledge currently dominant in Anglo-American philosophy tend to treat the nonpublic as nonobjective. Yet common sense can lead in a different direction. We frequently recognize expert knowledge that is not publicly verifiable, especially in fields having a marked aesthetic and stylistic dimension. In such sporting events as gymnastics, figure skating, surfing, and diving, for example, the score for the degree-of-difficulty of a performance is usually a publicly verifiable judgment based on the empirically observable sequence of movements. Given a detailed rulebook and a videotape of the performance, even a novice to the field should be able to determine such a score. For the quantitative evaluation of the style or form for the same performance, however, the spectators and performers defer to the judges' intimate knowledge. Still, we do not consider the evaluation of style to be merely a matter of subjective taste. In the event of a great discrepancy among the judges' decisions, we often suspect that political motivations have compromised objectivity. Normally we expect less than 5 percent deviation in the judges' scores—more than that and we suspect dishonesty. But such dishonesty, we should note, applies only to presumably objective judgments, not to subjective opinions.

We can distinguish this form of expert knowledge from the subjective expertise displayed by, say, a film critic. With film critics, we expect disagreement. Their judgment may include a factor as fickle as whether the critic liked the movie's theme, for example. Such an evaluation is inherently more subjective than that of a judge scoring a figure skating performance. In fact, if we read the opposing reviews of two critics, we feel justified in seeing the film and making our own judgment. This example shows that although we grant some expertise to the film critics, we still feel there is room for our own (subjective) judgment. On the other extreme, when a gymnastic judge determines whether the player stepped out of bounds during a free exercise performance, the basis of this decision is public, not private. If the television camera happens to have been properly placed, the videotape will conclusively prove the official's judgment right or wrong. This contrasts with the judge's rating the figure skater's form: no publicly accessible videotape can prove the performance was a 5.8 rather than a 5.7, for example. Unlike the film critic's evaluation, the gymnastic judge's ruling about the endline and the evaluation of form are both objective—we expect agreement to some degree. Yet in one case the judgment is verifiable publicly by anyone; in the other, only another expert is qualified to judge.

My third case exemplifies a complex of intimate and empirical knowledge. Most physicians would insist that diagnosis is as much an art as a science. In saying this, they mean they cannot always arrive at an accurate diagnosis simply by feeding a list of symptoms into a computer. There is more involved than just the empirically available facts. To diagnose a case, the physician must evaluate the scientific data in light of how the patient acts and speaks. (Is the patient a hypochondriac who exaggerates symptoms? A stoic who strives to ignore pain? A self-appointed expert who tries to make the symptoms fit the diagnosis? A likely candidate for a psychogenic disorder?) In traditional practice, physicians generally knew a great deal about their patients: their family situations, personalities, and habits. In other words: they were able to make medical judgments drawing on their intimate knowledge of the patient as well as the empirical knowledge gained from lab reports. It is significant that today, when our technical diagnostic devices are most sophisticated, we find a revival of the family practice system. The motive may be primarily an attempt at controlling costs, but it also suggests that physicians are more than technicians. The family physician consciously depends on forms of knowledge beyond those publicly verifiable in the simplistic scientific sense.

Let us sum up our discussion of intimacy's personal character. In everyday life, people often justifiably trust intimate forms of knowing that cannot be publicly verified but are still, in a significant sense, objective. It is important to distinguish, therefore, between two species of objectivity. The objectivity of publicly verifiable knowledge is based on empirical evidence and logic—that is, on what is immediately available to anyone (or at least anyone who has the necessary instruments and knows how to use them). Intimate knowledge's objectivity, by contrast, is accessible only to those within the appropriate intimate locus, those who have achieved their expert knowledge through years of practical experience. Trust in intimate knowledge's objectivity, like that in positivistic knowledge's objectivity, relies on an assumption of universality, but the universality has a somewhat different formulation. That is: if we believe that any reasonable person *who spent thirty years in gymnastics* would come to the same evaluation as the gymnastic judges, then we believe their judgment is objective, though not publicly so. The universality assumption of positivism differs only in omitting the italicized phrase, making the objectivity "public" rather than "expert." The common core of the objectivity claim in both public and nonpublic knowledge, however, is in their common phrase "any reasonable person." If I am making a merely subjective claim, I am not assuming possible agreement from every reasonable person. In a subjective judgment, reasonable people are expected to disagree; in an objective judgment, however, the expectation is that reasonable people either agree or at least can follow a procedure so that they will eventually agree. Similarly, we would be justified in thinking that if we spent decades studying, listening to, and performing Beethoven's sonatas, we could— like other experts—discern a difference in quality among them. Indeed, like Aunt Bessie, we could probably know what Uncle Herman was thinking if we too had lived with, and loved, the old codger for forty years. There is an objective quality to her knowledge.

## INTIMACY AS "BELONGING-WITH"

Intimacy is not merely personal, but personal in a special way. When in the locus of intimacy, one feels he or she *belongs* there. Among those persons, places, and things with which I am in intimate relation, I am comfortable, I feel at home and at peace. Outside the locus of intimacy, I sometimes sense I do not belong. I can sometimes be amidst my surroundings without feeling part of them, thinking of myself as something separate that has entered, and been forced to relate to, an alien environment. Even in my contacts with other people, I can distinguish the sense of "I-you" or "I-Thou" from the sense of "we." This point can be further clarified through the philosophical distinction between external and internal relations.

In an external relation, the relatents (the things in relation to each other) exist independently. As the link between these otherwise separate entities, the relationship *(R)* is in effect something added to the individuality of the things *(a)* and *(b)*. See Figure 8. In an internal relation, by contrast, it is part of the essential nature of the relatents that they are connected as they are; they are interdependent, not independent, entities.

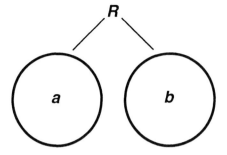
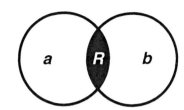

FIGURE 8. External Relation          FIGURE 9. Internal Relation

The internal relation *(R)* is part of both things *(a)* and *(b)*. See Figure 9.* To dissolve an internal relationship would not merely disconnect them; it would actually transform an aspect of the relatents themselves.

We experience intimate relations as internal rather than external. This is another way of saying that in my intimate relations I express what is innermost to me. That is: my intimate relations are more than connections I have made; they are actually part of what I am or have become. For example, for many years I was a student taking classes from various teachers. Those who impressed me most profoundly also influenced my own style of teaching: my style reflects their techniques and mannerisms. My close relationship to certain mentors has become part of what I am. In a similar vein, recall the example of the chess master, mathematician, and military historian and their different strategies for finding a seat on a crowded train. In such instances, their intellectual subject matter has become part of their everyday experience and view of life.

So if I were to lose anything with which I am in intimate relation—my family, my close friends, my home, even my dog-eared reference books—I would lose more than something I have. I would be losing part of myself. The differences between belonging-with and belonging-to are crucial to understanding this aspect of intimacy. In the preceding chapter we

---

*Throughout this book, diagrams like Figure 9 may remind philosophers of the Venn diagrams used in set theory. In many respects, this is not a problem. In analyzing the intimacy orientation, however, when we use a diagram like Figure 9 intimacy may consider the *a* and the *b* to be single entities that overlap. Normally a Venn diagram would not be construed as depicting the intersection of two sets, each of which has only one member. As I will explain in chapter 4, this disparity derives from a fundamental difference between the intimacy and integrity orientations.

had the example of the stolen wallet. If this had happened to me, both my money and my irreplaceable family pictures would be gone. The money belonged *to* me because I held temporary title to it (an external relation). The pictures, however, belonged *with* me (an internal relation) as a reminder accompanying me in my daily activities. In stealing the pictures, the thief stole something of myself, something to which I felt internally, not externally, related.

To bring the phenomenon of belonging into sharper focus, let us consider one final example. Few events in life are more painful than going through the belongings of a recently deceased loved one. Even the person's house or apartment seems transformed. The unfinished volume with the bookmark still in it, the favorite chair, the jewelry worn only on special occasions—all have a different significance. Like the dog moping in the kitchen, all these things seem to be waiting for the dead person to return home. It is as if the living friends and relatives have died also.

Of course, if we seek public verification that the house, the chair, and the jewelry have all changed in some way, we will find no empirical evidence of any transformation in the things themselves. The strong sense of belonging that we have singled out is not public. It is known only to those within the locus of intimacy. Only the person who had a close relationship with the deceased, therefore, would sense the change. But as we noted in our analysis of the personal dimension of intimacy, there is an objectivity to this perception. *Anyone* who had this close relationship with the deceased, anyone who was really within this locus of intimacy, would perceive the same sense of loss in the person's belongings and "personal effects." As this phrase implies, by entering into an intimate relationship with a thing we affect it personally.

Of course, the positivist may still think of this as gibberish because no scientific instrument can discern a change in the physical things. To this criticism we can make two replies. First: no empiricist can deny the observable change in the *behavior* of the close friends and relatives toward the deceased's belongings. The way they pet the dog, touch the jewelry, and affectionately pat the back of the chair are visible alterations of their usual behavior in relation to the things. At the same time, outsiders to the inner circle do not act in this way. Say, for example, the chair by the fireplace used to be Mom's chair. Since Mom has just died, its innermost character has been changed; its internal relationship with Mom has been disturbed. The objective, nonpublic aspect of the relationship can be easily discerned, for instance, when a comparative outsider at the reception after the funeral sits in what used to be Mom's chair. The members of the inner circle all find the situation odd and uncomfortable, whereas those outside the circle do not see anything strange or inappropriate in the act. That everyone in the inner circle senses the awkwardness of the situation is an indication of the objective relation between the chair and Mom. That not everyone in the room can sense this awkwardness is a sign of the nonpublic nature of the objectivity. There is, in short, an empirically discernible difference between how members and nonmembers of the intimate locus treat the dead person's belongings.

Second: even if hard-nosed empiricists grant the observable difference in the actions of the inner circle of intimates, they may still deny that the jewelry itself, for example, is in any way transformed. The members of the inner circle, however, might well question the metaphysical view that the jewelry can be understood as a thing-in-itself instead of a thing-in-relation. By considering the jewelry as "jewelry," the empiricist has already grouped together under a single category all the elements of the gems, the gold chains and clasps, the physically discrete pieces, and even the social use of the minerals as decorative adornments. The people in the dead woman's locus of intimacy, however, would differ only in including the person-to-whom-the-jewelry-belonged as part of the list of characteristics relevant to describing the jewelry. If it had not been for her, in fact, the discrete pieces of stone and gold would not be together in the box so that they could be classified as "the jewelry." Because they were all her belongings, they belong together in that particular jewelry box. From this perspective, the death of the person is as much a transformation of the jewelry as the tarnishing of the silver would be. Indeed, the probate court will recognize the legal status of the belongings and determine its new disposition ("dis" + "position": placing it apart from where it has been, where it had formerly belonged).

## INTIMACY AS AFFECTIVE

It is common today in modernist Western cultural contexts to think of emotion or feeling as distinct from knowing. This is generally legitimate. Much needless suffering derives from not being aware of the point where rationality ends and feelings begin—of the difference between what is and what one desires to be. Emotionalism is the enemy of reason. This is a valuable way of construing rationality, but it has inherent limitations.

Many of life's most anguishing decisions are not resolvable on logical and empirical grounds alone. One may gather all available facts, eliminate all spurious arguments, and still fail to reach a conclusion. You may still not know, for example, whether to institutionalize a severely handicapped child, when to volunteer advice about a friend's personal problem, or how much autonomy and responsibility to give to your son. Many decisions require not only logic and factual information, but also an imagination and conjecture nourished by experience. Experience, especially expert experience, can undergird rational hunches, suspicions, and intuitions. Such phenomena often involve feelings.

For a full understanding of intimacy, we need to analyze an affective form of imagination—namely, empathy. The golden rule, for example, requires people to think and feel as if they were the other person. Such an empathic imagination may, in fact, be necessary to full moral development. People often try to instill it in their misbehaving children by asking, "How would you like it if someone did that to *you?*" In so doing, they are asking the child to imagine being someone else and to feel what this imagined person would feel. Similarly, gracious hosts try to imagine and anticipate the needs and desires of their guests just as the servant tries to anticipate the needs of the master or mistress. In either case the goal is to anticipate the other person's requirements so that explicit requests or orders can be avoided or, at least, minimized.

When based on the empathic imagination, knowledge is generally transmitted or taught in a nondiscursive way. That is: the content and rules of an intimate form of knowing are of secondary importance to the practical training under a master or expert. After the technical training in medical school, the doctor serves apprenticeship as an intern or resident. During this time the physician is learning by imitating. But the imitating is not merely on the mechanical level of know-how. It involves the imaginative attempt to think, feel, and act like the role models. It resembles the acquisition of an art.

If we consider how we come to know a thing intimately, we find a similar approach. In my learning to use the ax to split firewood, for example, it was much simpler to learn the skill directly from an expert than to read a book on woodchopping. The proper feel of swinging the ax could be better communicated by showing than by describing. By watching my neighbor, I became sensitive to the design of the tool: the shape of the head, the balance of the handle, and so on. It would be pressing the point to say I empathized with the ax, but at least I imagined the feel of using the ax correctly as I watched my neighbor's demonstration. If we do want an example of empathizing with a thing, we can recall the story of Michelangelo's *David* as related in the preceding chapter. As the sculptor, Michelangelo felt that he had only made manifest what was already latently there in the stone.

In short: we find that empathic imagination can play an important role in the development of morality, technical skill with a tool, and aesthetic sensitivity. In all these cases, there is not only empirical observation and logical reasoning; there is also an emotive identification with a person or the use of an object. The presence of this affective dimension in intimacy should not surprise us after our analysis of intimacy as belonging. The sense of belonging is as much a feeling for, as a rational analysis of, an essential connection. Furthermore, belonging can suggest one's belonging with a particular group. That is: the feeling aspect of intimacy is not just a highly personalized, individualistic sense or a straightforward projection of one's own preferences. It also involves mirroring the feelings of one's group. It is not surprising, then, that a color scheme felt to be appropriate in one culture may be thought garish in another. The point is that within the given group—in this case, a cultural group—there is a common agreement instilled in children from an early age when they are instructed how to coordinate colors. To the people involved, to the people within the circle of intimacy (however this circle may be defined), the feeling eventually seems more objective than subjective. To clarify this point, let us consider another example.

Suppose a sportswriter's account claims "a feeling of gloom filled the locker room after the team's defeat." This may be considered no more than a metaphor, a rhetorical device not to be taken literally. Certainly one cannot validate the claim scientifically by using a gloomometer of some sort to test the room for unusual physical effects. To the emotionally detached observer, the people in the room look gloomy, but the room itself is unchanged. The room is incapable of feeling; it is completely indifferent to the fate of the team. There is no gloom discernible in the fluorescent lights overhead or in the picture of the superstar athlete hanging on the inside of the team captain's locker door.

So far, so good. But what if we were to abandon the detached analysis that views the room as something externally related to the team and were to try instead to see it as internally related to the team? The locker room would no longer simply be the room the team happens to be in: for the team members, or for anyone else who can empathetically imagine oneself a team member, it is part of the team's identity; it is the *team* locker room. Of all the loci in the universe, this one place is where the team as team belongs. On these fluorescent light fixtures are the spots from the champagne that was popped open only last week after the play-off victory. The light fixture is buzzing now. In fact, it has been buzzing for months, but nobody noticed it before. Right now, though, it is the only sound of which many players are aware. The team captain gazes at the picture in the locker—a talisman always given a pat for good luck just before the game. It is now only a slick, fragile, somewhat crumpled piece of paper stuck to the inside of the battleship gray locker door. By imagining oneself into the locus of intimacy defining the team, the "gloom-filled locker room" is no longer a mere metaphor. Rather, it accurately describes the team locker room from within the players' communal perspective. If one is restricted to the detached observer's standpoint, one cannot know this significance of the room as the team directly experiences its internal relation with it.

## INTIMACY AS SOMATIC

One goal of this discussion has been to help us think about intimate relations and intimate knowledge as something other than just sexual intimacy. We must be careful, however, not to exclude the somatic aspect completely. Even when intimacy is not carnal (and usually it is not), it is still incarnate. That is: human intimacy is embodied. The urge to put volume two next to volume one on the bookshelf is felt as a tension in the arm as well as an idea in the mind. The experience of the players' gloom-filled locker room is inseparable from both the sensory (sights, sounds, smells) and the visceral (the hollow feeling in the pit of the abdomen).

In noting the affective aspect of intimacy, it should not be surprising to find such a somatic component. After all, emotions are lived through the body. Whereas some have argued for the possibility of disembodied ideas, it is hard to imagine feeling a disembodied emotion. What would it mean to feel angry without a palpitating heart, tensed muscles, and a flushed face? What would fear be without cold, sweaty palms and shallow breathing? Sorrow without a tightness in the throat and heaviness in the chest? This is not to say that an emotion is nothing but a feeling—only that in most cases it would be difficult to think of emotions as independent of feelings.

What, then, is the precise relation between intimacy and the body? We have already noted that intimacy is an incorporating: a drawing into the body. This is intimacy in its etymological sense of *innermost*. We enter into intimate relations by opening ourselves to let the other inside, by putting ourselves into internal relations with others or recognizing internal relations that already exist. In the log-splitting example, I had to let the design of the ax affect my inner intentions. I had to feel the weight of the axhead as I gave it just enough of a push to start it on its arc. My change in attitude and posture made it possible for the ax to become an extension of my arms. My inner intent, the bodily movement, and the log-splitting design of the ax became, in effect, a single function.

The log-splitting example brings us to another dimension of the somatic aspect of intimacy—namely, its relation to praxis. By "praxis" I mean a pattern of practical behavior enacting a preconceived model. Praxis is fundamental to intimacy in two respects. First, in cases wherein intimacy involves a person, the intimate relation itself is established only through praxis. A person may theorize endlessly about the design and function of the ax, but until the ax is actually being used properly, the relation between the person and the ax is not yet intimate. In this sense, intimacy must be physically enacted.

The second point about praxis is that the intimacy deepens as the praxis is repeated or habitualized. That is: after getting the right idea about—indeed the right *feel* for—log splitting I established a proper posture and imitated the correct movements. At first there was some hesitancy and awkwardness as I tried to synchronize intent and action. But through practice, the correct movements became automatic and less self-conscious. Indeed, they became *second nature:* an acquired pattern of behavior became part of my inner nature, part of my own personal style. In short: my intimate relation with the ax is reflected, at least in part, in the posture and movements of my body.

Let us manage a further stage in this log-splitting example. Suppose I stop just as I am about to split a log because I see an unusual pattern in its grain. I put it aside and later take to chiseling a figurine out of that piece of hardwood. My intimacy with the log has moved from a merely technological relation to a deeper, more artistic expression. Like Michelangelo's experience with the block of marble discussed in chapter 1, the figurine is an expression of this piece of hardwood as much as it is an expression from me. I sensed, as it were, the wood's intimation of what it "wanted to be" and entered into a reciprocal expression with it. The figurine became an end-in-itself instead of a modification of nature for my immediate needs. We will discuss the artistic sensitivity of intimacy in chapter 5.

We have treated the somatic aspect of the intimate relation between logsplitter and ax or chiseler and hardwood—that is, between a person and a nonperson. What about the intimate relation between two people? How does the somatic structure articulate itself? What is the praxis involved? The basic structure is fundamentally similar to the artistry model but more complex: because both relatents are persons, both take the risk and make the commitment of incorporating and being incorporated. We could say, in fact, that both persons are artists and their intimacy itself is the work of art. Let us see how this is so.

First, let us not confuse the deeper senses of interpersonal intimacy with interpersonal manipulation. Despite what some sex manuals might suggest, intimacy is not achieved through the mastery of technical skills. To focus on technique is merely a form of social engineering or behavior modification: strategies for winning friends and influencing people or the how-to of being more effective in singles bars. In contrast, the purpose of establishing genuinely intimate relationships with others is, as in artistry, the intimate relationship itself. To treat a person otherwise is simply, as any Kantian would observe, to treat a person as a means instead of an end, as a tool to be used to achieve a practical benefit, instead of as an internal partner in the locus of intimacy. An intimate relation must be established as an end in itself, not a means to satisfying an ulterior motive: the improvement of one's social status, the advancement of one's position on the corporate ladder, the enhancement of one's sex life, or even the abatement of one's own loneliness, for example.

Only when we enter a relationship for the creative aspect of the relationship itself are we on the way to intimacy. The artistry of interpersonal intimacy, insofar as it leads to an internal relationship between two people, involves an opening up, a sharing, a belonging-with. And here is the challenge of interpersonal intimacy. To reach the ultimate goal of an intimate relationship, I must express to the other what is innermost. In so doing, I lay myself open, just like a nonhuman object, to being used as a tool. If my partner violates our mutual commitment and trust, I may become a mere instrument for her or his egoistic goals. But if my partner lives up to our promise, we both become a means to forming a transindividual internal relationship. Only by opening ourselves and trusting that the other will not violate our mutual commitment can we become part of each other. Such is the artistry of interpersonal intimacy.

This is still rather abstract, however. How exactly does a close personal relationship actually take form? And what is the somatic function? Contrary to the idiom, in our personal encounters there is no meeting of the minds. I meet not minds but people—flesh and blood, thinking and feeling, human beings. In other words: I encounter, first and always, an *incarnate* person, even if that person is only perceivable as a voice on a phone or a style of writing. When I love people, I cherish the chance to be in their physical presence. When I deeply dislike them, I hate their very looks. Originally people have no access to the other person's mind. This access comes only through the praxis of interpersonal intimacy. What establishes our initial interpersonal contact is our perception of the other person's style: the way one walks, talks, dresses, smiles, and so on. Even what the other person says cannot be sharply separated from the saying of it. To fathom a person's style, therefore, is to discover what is second nature to that person. Style intimates what is innermost to our personalities. To perceive a person's style is to learn the web of the person's intimate relations. While I am doing this, the other person is doing the same. By trying to read each other's intimations and by intimating ourselves, we seek the intrinsic interconnectedness that constitutes the basis of intimate relationship. As the idiom correctly states: we are *discovering what we have in common*. This common ground, this discovered overlap, is the very definition of internal relatedness.

Of course, interpersonal relationships are initially a morass of misinterpretations, the stuff of Shakespearean comedies and TV sitcoms. It is easy, at first, to misread the other person's conscious and unconscious signals. Learning to understand the other person's intimations is the praxis of intimate interpersonal relations. I try to fathom the other person's feelings; I try to hint how I myself feel. This exchange is the epitome of empathic imagination. We feel each other out. Certainly this "feeling" is primarily emotive, not tactile. The search for intimacy involves, as we have seen, both trust and the risk of losing privacy. Even in the most platonic type of relation, however, the feeling does involve a bodily physicality. "We feel each other out" through our attempts at intimating our innermost selves. And intimations are always expressed through the body via gestures, postures, intonation, facial expressions, and ways of moving. Each person in the burgeoning relationship uses the indirect discourse of intimation to suggest a part of the nonpublic self. If the other person can read the intimation and respond to it appropriately, contact is made. The two people begin to sense that they share some essential, not directly verbalized, qualities. They share something deeper than can be expressed in the questionnaire for a computer dating service.

Again, trust and good faith are the key. It is perfectly possible that one person in the relationship may be intimating a false self—pretending to be what one is not. On one level, this may be coquettish teasing or macho posturing; on another, personal betrayal. In either case, the offended party feels exposed and violated. Sometimes the exposure may be only mildly embarrassing, perhaps even humorous like the Candid Camera television show where one can laugh along with the public at what one had thought was private. In more serious cases, it can be personally devastating to have your innermost self laid bare for all to see.

The somatic physicality of intimacy is sometimes literal, of course, expressing itself sexually. Under special conditions, this can be the natural consummation of a process that was, in a very different sense, somatic right from the start. The physical act of love is an incarnate acting out of the process of intimation: feeling, incorporation, sharing what is innermost, style, gesture, and movement are given the highest level of concreteness and directness. Of course, the lack of trust, the presence of bad faith, the waffling of commitment, the reduction of the other to a means instead of an end, and the imposition of technique over the artistry of relationship can rob this act of its primordial significance. And what is this primordial significance? It is the creative life of the intimate relationship as an end in itself. Again, this may even have a concrete embodiment: the most physical expression of sharing can become an end—a life—in its own right, a child born of the internal relationship itself and not of either individual alone.

Having discussed the somatic aspect of intimate relationships between persons and things as well as persons and persons, we need to say something about the most abstract of relations—that between a person and a set of concepts. How can there be a somatic dimension to a relation so idealized? If we return to our case of the chess master, mathematician, and military historian on the crowded train, the situation is not so puzzling. As we noted, detailed knowledge alone does not qualify as intimate knowledge. To have an intimate knowledge of something, a person must be impassioned about the subject. A computer's memory bank, however extensive, does not know something intimately. We expect the person with intimate knowledge to be absorbed, excited, and committed to the subject. These are all affective characteristics, and we would expect them to have physical manifestations in the individual's personal style. As Michael Polanyi pointed out in *Personal Knowledge,* even scientists participate personally in knowledge by committing themselves to a hypothesis and working out its verification or refutation in the laboratory. Thus even in science there is no such thing as a detached objective observer: the scientist, by being a scientist, is not disinterested in the results of an experiment. Furthermore, as suggested earlier, the chess master, mathematician, and the military historian all have their own personal style in finding a seat on the crowded train—a style that intimates their assimilation of a particular field of knowledge.

To sum up, then, we have investigated how intimate knowledge has a somatic dimension in at least two senses: it is achieved through praxis, and it is embodied through physical style. These two senses are often, in fact, related through the learning process itself. Once a computer has the information entered via the keyboard, there is no point in repetition. Human beings achieve intimate knowledge, however, through continuous exposure and reexposure. Ideas are forgotten only to be relearned in a different context. One remembers not only the lesson from class but also the affect embedded in the interpersonal style of the teacher. In fact, a truly intimate knowledge of something is almost invariably learned from a master's own intimate knowledge of the subject. The subject is learned through imitation of the teacher's thinking process. This process of imitation includes reading the intimations of the master and incorporating them into oneself. Thus the teacher's personal style—even some of the physical mannerisms—may be reincarnated, at least in part, by the disciple.

## INTIMACY AS DARK OR ESOTERIC

Intimacy's fifth characteristic is perhaps the most difficult to grasp. It suggests that intimacy itself is inscrutable, at least in one crucial respect. Yet as we shall see, this characteristic is consistent with what we have already discussed. By saying intimacy is "dark" I mean that the foundation or ground of intimate knowledge is not obvious even to those involved in the intimate locus. How I know my car needs fuel differs from how I know my child is worried about something. If I have been driving my car for some time without filling the tank and the gauge on my dashboard reads just above "empty," I know I need to get some gas. There is nothing puzzling or arcane about the grounds of this knowledge. In the case of my child's emotional state, however, I may not be so readily able to give the grounds for my knowledge. Perhaps I just sense that my son is "not his usual self." If you ask me what this means, I may not be able to specify the precise behavior that is atypical. If I am relatively intelligent, sensitive, and articulate, I may be able to do so after thoughtful reflection. But the significant point is that the basis of my judgment only becomes clear to me after thinking about the judgment I have already made. In short: in the case of knowing the status of my car's fuel tank, at the time of the judgment the grounds for the knowledge are as clear as the judgment itself. In the case of judging my son's psychological state, however, the ground is dark—at least until I later shed the self-conscious light of reflection on it.

The term "esoteric" adds another dimension to the darkness. Like the word "intimacy," this term has been co-opted by popular culture. As intimacy is frequently reduced to sexuality in common parlance, the esoteric has often been reduced to black magic, the occult, mystic experiences, even chicanery. I use the word to refer specifically to the context in which a nonpublic, but objective, insight is available only to members of a certain group who have undergone special training. In this sense, we commonly speak of the esoteric aspects of computer programming or furniture refinishing. In our sense, then, the esoteric is not necessarily secretive or exclusive. It is open to everyone who has entered the intimate circle. How does one do that? By undergoing the appropriate praxis.

To understand the significance of the dark and esoteric character of intimate knowledge, let us examine what may at first seem a trivial example. I have often witnessed a postgame sports interview like the following:

> "Hey, Eddie, you did it! With less than twenty seconds in the game, you broke loose and scampered thirty-five yards for the game-winning touchdown. Tell us about it, Eddie. How did you know when to break out of the set play and cut against the grain like that?"
>
> "Well, we started with a quick-opener on the right side. I made my cut and there was no hole. Then I saw some daylight on the other side, so I just took it."

What a disappointing answer! By watching the game on television, I already knew as much. I wanted Eddie to tell me *why* something happened, but he only described *what* happened. Until asked by the reporter, Eddie had never even thought about how he knew when to cut. The move was second nature to him: at the time of his heroics, he was neither self-conscious nor reflective. When asked his private thoughts and motives at the time of the great play, therefore, Eddie has nothing to tell us. He is in the dark.

Now suppose that Eddie, a bit embarrassed by his own simplistic answer, gives the question more thought. The next time he is asked, he responds as follows.

> "Do you mean how did I know where to look for daylight? Well, let's see. First of all, we practice that play maybe ten times a day. Our own defense, of course, has become pretty experienced at reading the play and reacting quickly to it. So in practice sessions, it's not unusual to find the expected hole clogged up and I guess I've formed the habit of always checking the opposite direction. Actually, then, I've probably made the same move I did today maybe a hundred times in practice.
>
> "Also, I guess I should add that the coach had us watch game films of our opponents for hours on end. I suppose I developed a feel for how they react to certain situations. Although I don't remember thinking about it at the time of the play, we did notice in the films that they sometimes overplay the blocks and leave themselves open to that kind of reverse, particularly late in the game when they're tired."

Certainly this description is more revealing. In fact, Eddie might make a very good sportscaster after he finishes his football career. But let's be more critical. With a few word changes, this description would apply equally well to almost any play by any participant in the game. Eddie has shifted from describing the play to describing the praxis of football training. If all players were as articulate about praxis as Eddie, I would soon get bored again with postgame interviews. Still looking for the uniqueness of the game-winning play, I would only be told about the general constants of football training.

Eddie's dilemma reveals an important point about the esoteric aspect of intimacy. The content of his intimate knowledge of football cannot be adequately described discursively in a step-by-step, logical manner. Wishing a full discursive account, we must settle for an account of the praxis used to initiate him into the intimate locus. That is: Eddie can explain how he became a football star, but not the special knowledge he achieved through that training. How does a pitcher know when to throw a change-up? How does a prosecuting attorney know when to press the witness further and when to back away? How does a teacher know what example will help the student? How does a parent know when a child is upset? One cannot exactly say. All we can do is explain the practical experience—perhaps the praxis guided by a master—that brought us to this intimate, esoteric knowledge. Indeed, if a completely satisfactory discursive account of the intimate content itself could be given, this would prove that the initiation was bogus—that the insight could have been communicated plainly even to someone who has not undergone the praxis. Why should Eddie even bother to go to practice if everything he needs to know can be found in a playbook?

Although the content of the intimate knowledge cannot be communicated adequately to an outsider, it can be suggested. To the one who remains an outsider, these might be vague conundrums but nothing more substantial. The insider, however, will immediately recognize them as intimations and know their ultimate significance. Returning to an earlier example, when anyone sees Uncle Herman's furrowed eyebrows, the assumption is that he is worried or concerned. Aunt Bessie, however, can see these same eyebrows and know just how worried or upset he is and perhaps even know what is troubling him. She may even sense a feeling Herman himself may not be able to verbalize. Incidentally, some outsiders may be more adept than others at interpreting Herman's intimations. A person with a highly developed empathic imagination or one who has undergone many life experiences similar to Herman's may be particularly receptive to Herman's cues. In other words: because of their special attunement, some people can more readily enter into a new locus of intimacy. The praxis of intimacy may carry over from one context to the next.

Note the difference between a discursive account of the praxis and practicing the praxis. When operatic singers have trouble controlling their voice, they go to voice coaches not music critics. The coach has an intimate knowledge of singing praxis and can direct the singer in the right therapy. The music critic, by contrast, can better interpret the voice problem to the general public, even though the critic may not know what remedy should be followed. In short: praxis is best learned from a master within the appropriate locus of intimacy. Even if the master cannot articulate completely the praxis' purpose, the master is best at intimating to an insider what should be done. What is dark and esoteric to an outsider may, when put into practice, be commonsensical to an insider.

In concluding this analysis of intimacy, let us relate this chapter to our general project of trying to achieve a cultural philosophy of relationship. As this chapter has shown, there is nothing particularly cultural about the experiences of intimacy itself. Intimacy is a human, not a cultural, phenomenon. What is significant for our purposes, however, is that one can at least imagine a culture that places a primary, rather than secondary, value on the enhancement of intimacy. Furthermore, one might be able to deduce what kind of philosophical orientation would flourish in such a culture. Before pursuing this project, however, let us turn to the contrasting orientation of integrity. Once we have analyzed this, we compare the two and see how they tend to articulate and analyze thought and value.

# CHAPTER 3

# WHAT IS INTEGRITY?

Having discussed intimacy in the previous chapter, we now turn our attention to the other relational orientation: integrity. "Integrity" is a foreground word in modern Western culture that suggests a virtue both solid and stolid. Extolled in the common phrases "having honesty and integrity," or "a person of integrity and character," or "integrity and honor," the word "integrity" has many nuances. Thus I need to specify its use here. In chapter 1, when considering its etymological roots, we found the term to suggest being whole, indivisible, and inviolable. What has integrity is untouched or pure. A person with integrity does not compromise her or his own virtue because of outside influence; like Eliot Ness' gangbusting crew of federal agents, such a person is "untouchable." If a dam has integrity, it is free from leaks and the likelihood of crumbling. In short: integrity means being able to stand alone, having a self-contained identity without dependence on, or infringement by, the outside.

Either things or persons may have integrity. Let us begin with integrity in things by considering how water is related differently to sand and to salt when it is in the ocean. Sand and seawater certainly influence each other. Sandbars affect the formation of waves and, in turn, the waves scoop up the sand from the bottom, hurl it ashore, and then pull it back out to sea. Yet the water and sand each maintains its own integrity. Though related, the seawater remains seawater and the sand remains sand. The ocean maintains its liquidity; the sand retains its crystalline solidity. The sand may be suspended in the water of the breaking wave, but it never changes its essential nature by becoming part of the water itself. Now consider the internal relation between the salt and water in the ocean. Where there is seawater, we find both water and salt, but only insofar as they are merged. The salt dissolves into the liquid water and the water itself becomes salty. Their independent identities as salt and water disappear into the single solution of seawater. The seawater is an intimate relationship between salt and water insofar as each surrenders part of its own nature—the crystalline salt and the pure water—in becoming part of the relational whole of the ocean. This relation contrasts with the sand's maintaining its crystalline wholeness however much it might be externally related to the seawater.

These relationships between salt and seawater as contrasted with sand and ocean fit the diagrams of internal and external relations from the previous chapter. In the internal, intimate relation of salt and seawater, their identities overlap. Salt is part of what the seawater is; ocean is part of the nature of sea salt. The sand, by contrast, has it own unchanging, intrinsic characteristics whether it is at the bottom of the ocean or in a sandbox. Similarly, the seawater is the same whether it is churning up in breakers of the Pacific Ocean or in a glass beaker in a laboratory. The relation between the seawater and the sand, therefore, is one of integrity, not intimacy. The intrinsic natures of the seawater and sand remain inviolable regardless of the relationships linking them. Their relationship is external, not internal. This discussion of integrity among things leads us to our consideration of integrity among persons.

In the case of persons, we have noted, integrity is usually considered a virtue. In whatever situation or relationship such people of integrity may find themselves, their self-identities are neither corrupted nor compromised. When people have integrity, we can count on them to be consistent with their previous behavior—responding to different contexts without being fundamentally changed by the contexts. We often say such people are "principled," that is, they believe in an external, often universal, set of values and standards they apply to different situations. The principles, not the situation, dictate the behavior. Even when a person of integrity undergoes a change, the change is in the principles to which this person feels a sense of duty. Principled people can change their behavior, but only by changing their principles or at least giving the principles different weight or interpretations than before.

Because of its untouchable character, integrity might at first seem not to be a relational term at all. Yet we seldom apply the term "integrity" to loners—to those who disconnect themselves from others. Contrary to the first impression, in fact, integrity only has meaning *within* relationship. Integrity is a mode of relating to others, one that maintains the self-identity of the related persons even while they are being related, similar to the water and the sand of the ocean. I recognize a person's integrity only as I observe that person in relationships. Just as the seawater and sand do not dissolve into each other, in an integrity relationship between people the individuals connect to each other and interact without either one becoming even partially identified with, or absorbed into, the other. As the diagram of external relations suggests (Figure 8), integrity maintains the space between the relatents even as it bridges the gap.

This analysis of integrity suggests that a person of integrity is not simply an individual, but an individual-in-relation. Often there is confusion on this point because people of integrity maintain their own identities regardless of that to which they relate. Because people of integrity will maintain their identity even in the face of external pressure—they will stick to their principles whatever the coercion—the person of integrity seems the "same" in all circumstances and, therefore, seems the paradigm of the individual. This is only part of the story, however. A person of integrity not only remains inviolate *from* infringements by the other; such a person also does not, in principle, violate the other person's identity. The person of integrity maintains the individuality of others as well as his or her own. In short: the individual's character as a person of integrity reveals itself fully only in relationship to others.

Having discussed integrity in terms of thing-to-thing and person-to-person, what can we say about the third possibility: person-to-thing? In this case, it is important that the person recognize the integrity of the object to which he or she relates. The thing has its own nature—its characteristic or essential qualities—that one must respect. Environmental ethics, for example, may proceed from an orientation that the integrity of the ecosystem should not be transgressed—that the environment has its own inviolable "rights." In this line of thought, it is sensible to say that nature does not exist *essentially* as something for human use: it has its own internal raison d'être; it exists, in an important sense, for itself. Yet humans may still use nature if they respect its integrity—if they see the use as a contract rather than an assault. Humanity has the *responsibility* to interact with nature in a way that preserves nature's intrinsic character. (As we will see in chapter 5, "responsibility" is an integrity concept.)

Chapter 5 explores environmental ethics in both its intimacy and integrity orientations.

## FIVE ASPECTS OF INTEGRITY

In the preceding chapter, we analyzed intimacy in terms of five characteristics. Here it is instructive to reexamine these characteristics as contrasting with the characteristics of integrity.

### Integrity as Impersonal

First we noted that intimacy supports an expert form of knowledge that is objective but not publicly verifiable by those outside the locus of intimacy. For intimacy, understanding is often restricted to those whose praxis makes them "in the know." Integrity, by contrast, emphasizes knowledge based on empirical observation and logical reasoning, both of which can be verified by anyone else, at least theoretically. If the cup is on the table, this fact is theoretically knowable by anyone. For integrity, it is irrelevant who happens to see it as such—irrelevant who makes this visual experience the basis of a true judgment. Rhetorically this leads to a depersonalization of statements: "one" knows rather than "I" know or "we" know. Public verifiability, not the expert, is the basis of authority.

The emergence of philosophical modernism and the ensuing Enlightenment tradition in Western thought included an increasing emphasis on the integrity orientation in terms of knowledge. We find this clearly in the principles of legal justice, for example. Whereas legal decisions were once exclusively in the hands of ecclesiastical or political authorities, they now rest, in theory at least, in the public statement of law and in adjudication guided by clearly defining principles. The Enlightenment condemned judgments by fiat as a violation of the defendant's integrity—the person's inherent "rights." In principle, no personal authority, no matter how powerful, is entitled to punish a person without proof of guilt. To preserve the integrity of the accused, accusations in court now require publicly verifiable evidence. Such evidence must be deemed publicly objective—that is, it is accessible to disinterested, nonexpert parties such as a group of one's peers. Nor does integrity recognize guilt by mere association. Within the context of integrity, the individual may be in relation to another without being corrupted by that other. Before God and before the law, integrity dictates that the person stand alone in her or his own virtue or vice and be judged accordingly. To deny a person this status is a violation of that person's rights: the person's untouchable boundaries have been penetrated and there is defilement of what should be preserved as essential and inalienable.

The tenet of publicly verifiable evidence is also the principle behind the requirement that scientific experiments be replicable. In the integrity orientation, people do not simply take the word of a scientist, not even a Nobel Prize winner, unless that scientist's claims can be confirmed by others who can duplicate the same experiments with the same results. In such a context, the idiom is that the "evidence speaks for itself." That is, it has own integrity and stands independent of who performs the experiment. There is no room in modern Western science for either priest or magician. The truth cannot depend on who discovers it or articulates it. Where the integrity orientation is dominant, objectivity must always be public and expert knowledge is often viewed with suspicion as a cloaked appeal to some esoteric authority. We will have the opportunity to explore such issues further in the next chapter when we discuss epistemology.

### Integrity as "Belonging-To"

The second characteristic of intimacy is that it involves a "belonging-with" rather than integrity's "belonging-to." Let us return to our diagrams as an aid in seeing how belonging-to is an external relation whereas belonging-with is internal. In Figure 10, suppose $b$ represents $a$'s

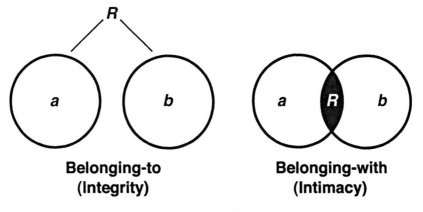

FIGURE 10. Belonging-to and Belonging-with

belongings. In the integrity orientation, belongings are understood as one's possessions ($a$ is the owner; $b$ is the property; $R$ is the external relation establishing $a$'s ownership of $b$). In such an understanding, $a$ "holds title" ($R$) over $b$ and can do with $b$ as he or she pleases (so long as one does not violate the integrity of other people). This external relationship of belonging-to contrasts with what we saw in chapter 2 as intimacy's understanding of belongings as personal effects. (The internal relation $R$ represents $b$'s overlap with $a$, making $b$ into $a$'s personal effects.) Such intimate belongings are part of one's identity insofar as they collectively intimate who I am: my style. If I find the appropriate item of clothing, for example, I might exclaim, "It's me!" It belongs *with* me, rather than *to* me.

When thinking in terms of integrity and inquiring into a relation between $a$ and $b$, I typically ask "what connects the two?" In doing so, I am asking what $R$ is—an $R$ that is not itself $a$ or $b$ but instead something that associates $a$'s integrity with $b$'s integrity. If the relation is broken or dissolved, $a$ is still $a$ and $b$ is still $b$. In other words: if $a$ and $b$ enter into a relation $R$, $a$ and $b$ are essentially unchanged. The relation is something $a$ and $b$ possess; it is something external that belongs *to* them. Of course, this externality does not mean that the relationship has nothing at all to do with the character of $a$ and $b$. If $a$ chooses to be in the relation $R$ with $b$, for example, this indeed reflects something about $a$'s own nature. That is: $a$ has the intrinsic character to seek external relations of the sort $R$ with entities like $b$ (or vice versa). As we will see in chapter 5, such a mode of thinking can lead to a social contract model of political philosophy. Such a theory claims that the nature of human beings leads to establishing certain appropriate kinds of external, contractual relations with others.

In an intimacy orientation, by contrast, in analyzing a relation between $a$ and $b$ I may ask "what is the relationship between the two?" or "what do they have in common?" To understand $a$, I necessarily understand something of $b$ as well. By inquiring into their relationship, I find the point of commonality or overlap that $a$ and $b$ share (instead of an external $R$ that connects them). Because $b$ is partly $a$ and vice versa, they belong *with* (not *to*) each other. Sometimes we suggest this difference by saying in the integrity orientation that "$a$ has relations with $b$, $c$, $d$" whereas in the intimacy orientation we might say "$a$ is interrelated with $b$, $c$, $d$." The language suggests that in an integrity orientation $a$ is a discrete entity that gets connected with other entities, but in an intimacy orientation $a$ has its relatents as part of its own identity. Returning to the

Latin roots of the words, in an external relation *a* is an indivisible, pure entity *(integer)*. In understanding *a* as internally related, by contrast, we discover something about what is "innermost" *(intimus)* to it—namely, its overlap with *b*.

This difference becomes even clearer when we consider the result of a dissolved or broken relationship in both orientations. Figure 11 shows the progression of what happens when *a* and *b* enter into relations of intimacy and integrity and then what happens when these relations disappear or are broken. With the termination of an external relationship (that is, with the erasure of the *R* connecting the relatents), the *a* and *b* maintain

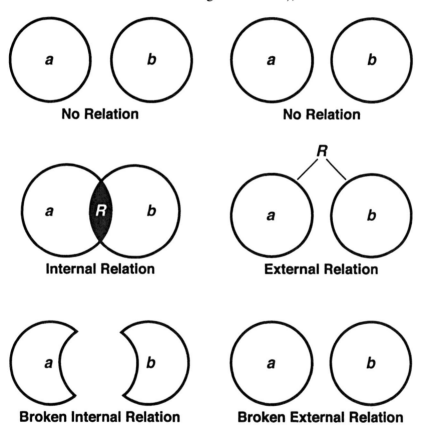

**a.** Intimacy Orientation    **b.** Integrity Orientation

FIGURE 11. Formation and Dissolution of Internal and External Relations

their integrity and exist as unbroken, unviolated, wholes. Terminating an internal relationship, by contrast, results in both relatents losing a part of their identity: the *a* and *b* become less themselves or at least less of what they had been.

To differentiate the two kinds of belonging, it is instructive to consider the difference between marriage as a legal relationship and marriage as a love relationship. One reason why marriage has a legal status is to pre- serve the integrity of the people establishing the relationship. Therefore, if the legal relationship is dissolved, the law protects against the violation of the integrity of either *a* or *b*. Each is entitled to certain legal rights and obligations incurred at the time of marriage and operative at its dissolu- tion (in divorce, death, or whatever). When marriage is viewed as a love relationship, however, it more resembles an internal relationship. In the loss of the loving marriage, one literally loses part of oneself.

It follows that people understand themselves differently in the two cul- tural orientations. In an integrity orientation (see Figure 12), my identity

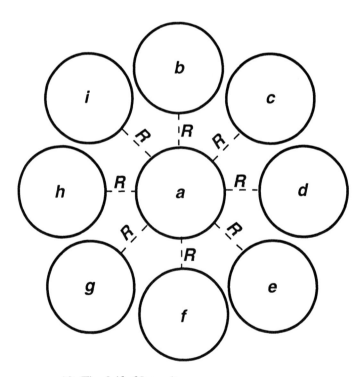

FIGURE 12. The Self of Integrity

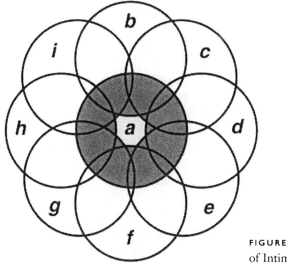

FIGURE 13. The Self of Intimacy

corresponds with the fixed boundaries of the ego *(a)*. Although I see myself connected to many other things, none of these things is literally part of me. In this context, to "find myself" means to discover who I am independent of external factors. This may lead to a strong sense of autonomy. My relationships are not what I am, but that to which I have independently *chosen* to be connected. I am in control, at least theoretically, of how (and often to what) I relate.

Because intimacy involves a necessary connection with others (either people or things), my identity in the intimacy orientation *(a)* necessarily overlaps with what is outside the discrete ego (the full-circled *a,* both the shaded and open parts, in Figure 13). Rather than the independence of integrity, intimacy favors interdependence. In an intimacy orientation, to "find myself" means that I see how I am interconnected with, and interdependent with, many other entities. My self-discovery discovers the interdependence defining my life. The contrast between these two views of the self is clearly visible in the differences between existentialism and Buddhism.

Existentialism, for instance, emphasizes integrity and autonomous freedom. For the existentialist the freedom of choice is always framed by "facticity"—the external circumstances over which one has no control. Yet the existentialist maintains, no matter how restrictive the facticity, there is always room for some autonomy. In his *Myth of Sisyphus,* for example, Albert Camus relates the classical myth of a man condemned by the gods to eternal torment. Assigned the task of rolling a boulder up a hill, Sisyphus continuously tries to do so. But as he approaches the very top, the rock always rolls back down. It is hard to imagine a more restrictive and demoralizing circumstance. Yet as Camus points out, the gods may be able to control Sisyphus' physical situation but they cannot control how he feels about it. Camus portrays Sisyphus as giving a defiant grin each time he has to start over. In Camus's integrity orientation, Sisyphus is in an external relation to his predicament. He cannot choose his task; he cannot control his circumstance. But this "*circum*-stance" is just that—what stands *around* him but not *in* him. He can still define his identity by controlling his way of relating to these circumstances. Sisyphus' attitude is his own. No external situation can infringe on it unless he lets it. As the idiom goes, he does not let the gods "get into his head." He remains untouchable in his integrity. Sisyphus maintains external relations $(R)$ with the facticity around him ( $b-i$ in Figure 12). He defines the nature of R even though he cannot control the circumstances $(b-i)$ to which these relations connect him. By keeping the relations external, however, he is able to maintain the integrity of self $(a)$. His true self is not violated.

Intimacy's view of the self, a view typically taken in Buddhism, is quite different. Because intimacy's self $(a)$ is in internal relation with the surrounding things and events, it may have an isolated core of identity (the unshaded section of $a$ in Figure 13). Most of $a$'s identity, however, is also shared by surrounding entities and events. In its traditional understanding of the self, Buddhism pushes the intimacy orientation to its furthest logical point. Buddhism entirely denies the existence of the "I" or ego (*ātman*) as an independent entity. The Buddhist understands *every* aspect of the Buddhist self to be conditioned by processes around him or her. In the Buddhist self's diagrammatic representation, there is no unshaded or independent part of $a$ left (see Figure 14). This lack of the independent ego—the lack of an unshaded part of $a$—is what Buddhists call *anātman*, "no ego" or "no-I." This does not mean that I am without identity; there is still the unique overlap of interdependent process defining who I am (as represented by the full circle of $a$). The major point for Buddhism, however, is that the overlaps defining $a$ are completely interdependent (completely shaded) and without any trace of independent substantiality—without any untouched nucleus.

According to Buddhism, therefore, I am not a self-existent being who

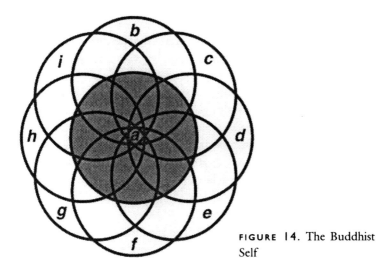

FIGURE 14. The Buddhist Self

chooses with what or how I wish to relate to external circumstances. Instead the sum total of my situation defines me. I *(a)* am the nexus of a series of completely interdependent processes *(b–i)* and the processes of which I am part lead me to connect with further processes. If *a* is internally related to *f,* for example, it is likely that *a* will relate internally to other processes internally related with *f.* In the intimacy model of self depicted in Figure 13, for example, *f* is related in this way with *d, e, g,* and *h.* In the Buddhist model depicted in Figure 14, though, *f* is internally related with *all* the other circles—that is, with *b* to *i.* This gives us an approximation of the Buddhist idea of dependent coproduction: every thing comes into being and ceases to exist only through its dependence on other things.

*Integrity as Purely Intellectual* _____

As explained in chapter 2, a third characteristic of the intimacy orientation is its emphasis on affect as well as intellect. Intimacy assumes that the self overlaps with its relations and, consequently, that it is possible for me to know something about things by drawing on my own inner resources. This looking inward, often called "introspection" or "intuition," can be affectively charged so that I get a feel for things without externalizing them. Consider Figures 13 and 14. When I *(a)* fully know myself in the intimacy orientation, I also know something of all that is internally related to me, namely, *b* to *i*. Within the integrity orientation, by contrast, the intellect is clearly dominant. I may have hunches or intuitions, but integrity trusts these affective aspects of knowledge only so far: they may suggest hypotheses to be subsequently tested by objective, public knowledge, but they can never have the full status of knowledge itself. By establishing external relations with things, integrity favors the viewpoint of the "objective observer." Integrity advises us "to think with our heads, not our heart," whereas intimacy allows that "in our hearts we know what is true." As portrayed in Figure 12, *a*'s knowledge of the world *(b–i)* only comes about by seeing what is related to, but outside, the self *(a)*. In the next chapter we will analyze some of the implications of this difference between intimacy's and integrity's view of knowing reality.

In the integrity orientation, people mistrust the emotions because feelings might confuse us about what we experience and how to interpret it. Emotions may lead us to see what we desire, instead of what actually is. Emotion may project part of my self into the world, personally coloring my perception. Integrity demands that I stand outside my ego and look at things as if I had no desire that they be one way or another. Because integrity insists on such an impersonal stance, anyone else who can view the situation equally dispassionately should see reality in the same way. The ideal observer does not violate or defile the way things are and therefore leaves them untouched for the next objective observer. In Figure 12 we could substitute any *x* for *a* and the known objects *b–i* would remain the same. This is not true for Figures 13 or 14, however. In these intimate contexts, if *a* changes, so too must *b–i*. This is why integrity requires public verification for its objectivity. If there is no such verification, there is a suspicion that judgment might have colored phenomena with personal affect. Integrity calls this affect "subjectivity." According to the integrity orientation, subjectivity takes part of my inner self and projects it into the world, giving it my personal construction. For the integrity orientation, knowledge—like its ideal of justice—is supposed to be blind, impartial, and impersonal.

*Integrity as Purely Conceptual* _____

As we saw in chapter 2, the fourth characteristic of intimacy follows from the third—namely, intimacy has a somatic as well as an intellectual component. Intimate knowledge is achieved through repetitive praxis, usually under the guidance of a master. Where integrity is dominant, however, intimacy's brand of expert knowledge is often considered no more than know-how or technique. For integrity, the highlighted kind of knowledge is the "knowing that" or "knowing why" based on principles and verifiable through public test. The principles guide the method that ascertains the laws of how things work. Therefore integrity insists that, at least theoretically, knowledge is open to anyone, not just to experts. With plainly articulated principles, people can settle disagreements through independent tests. In societies dominated by the integrity orientation, the public has a "right to know." This right is an extension of integrity's insistence that knowledge is publicly verifiable and that experts are not entitled to withhold information on the basis of "special knowledge." From the idea that knowledge can be shared we have moved to the idea that knowledge should be shared.

In short: integrity's basis for knowledge is fundamentally intellectual. This position differs radically from intimacy's claim that its form of knowledge can only be evaluated by experts who have embodied years of a disciplined, shared praxis. Rhetorically, intimacy often appeals, either positively or negatively, to an ad hominem form of argument. Those lacking the years of training and guided praxis are not given a voice in judgments. Such nonexperts cannot even access the knowledge because it is somatically as well as intellectually assimilated. One has to be an "insider" to know. In short: the persuasive tactic of the knower in an integrity context is "I will show you the evidence and explain my reasoning." In intimate circles, by contrast, the tactic is "become a disciple, engage in the praxis, and find out for yourself"—or, even in extreme cases, the exclusivist claim that "you can never understand because you are not one of us."

### Integrity as Bright and Open

This leads us to the fifth characteristic of intimacy and its contrast with integrity. Intimacy, we have seen, is "dark" or "esoteric"—that is, you cannot explain clearly to anyone (even yourself) the rational basis for your insight. Because it is as embedded in the accumulative experience of somatic praxis as in intellectual thought, intimate knowledge is inexplicable to those who have not undergone the appropriate praxis. It can be intimated, but not explicated. Yet as we have seen, in assuming that knowledge has its own integrity or inviolable nature independent of the knower's affect, the integrity orientation stresses principles against which one can test the claims to knowledge. With this acute sense of explicable self-consciousness, therefore, it is fair to say that integrity's knowledge is "bright" rather than "dark." It tries to "bring to light" the data and reasoning behind any claim to knowledge—both for oneself and to persuade others. Integrity seeks intellectual "illumination"; it tries to "shed light" on problems and their solutions; cartoonists depict a lit lightbulb to indicate an idea has "dawned" on the character. For integrity, knowledge is an open and public event. To know entails being able to explain the rationale and principles behind the knowledge.

## IMPLICATIONS

Having analyzed the chief differences between intimacy and integrity, we can now begin to explore their implications for philosophizing. How do intimacy and integrity operate as orientations within the cultural development of worldviews, modes of social interaction, and ways of self-understanding? As an introduction to how orientations construct meaning, in chapter 1 we examined a few simple gestalt pictures as examples of how alternative interpretations can develop from a change of focus on the same image. I suggested that a culture typically informs its members (through education, idioms, material culture, and so forth) about what is important, or what is to be foregrounded, in the complex array of phenomena. People of different cultures construct different meanings out of what could be construed, on one level, to be the same event.

To characterize the relation between cultural orientation and philosophy further, it is perhaps useful to resort to yet another analogy—in this case one from computer science rather than gestalt psychology. Indeed the function of cultural orientations in some ways parallels the function of the operating system and software in computers. Operating systems and cultures alike help to organize and bestow meaning on the astounding array of input received at any moment. They determine "what counts" and "where it belongs" in relation to the data already processed. My five external senses are receptors that operate continuously, filling my consciousness with a dazzling stream of sights, sounds, tastes, feelings, and smells. My internal receptors signal pangs of hunger, nausea, itches, pain, and so forth. My memories, imagination, and thought processes lend still further input to the array. To avoid chaos—to be able to survive—I cannot be a passive monitor of such micro-phenomena. Instead I must engage what is around me: organizing it, connecting the bits into something meaningful, and effectively ignoring or peripheralizing everything else. Some of this processing is autonomic and anatomic, hardwired into my neurological structures from the earliest stages of life. The sensation of searing heat, for example, causes a reflex to withdraw from the contact even before I consciously recognize the burning object and identify it as dangerous. Reactions to other signs of danger—the rattle of a snake, the buzz of a hornet's nest, the sound of an oncoming truck—have to be acquired (or even rewired) through a process of learning, perhaps through the guiding clasp of a parent's hand. I also need to learn about contexts: the combined sensation of flickering light, heat, and the smell of smoke requires different responses depending on whether I experience it around a campfire or in the hayloft of a barn. More complex interpretive-reactive structure develops as I acquire skill in understanding symbolic signs: interpreting the warning label on a household chemical product, the red glow of a traffic signal, or a map.

One can arrange these processes of structured response in a spectrum —from the reflex reaction to burning heat on one end of the scale to the reading of signs on the other. As we move along this spectrum, we find that culture plays an increasingly important role. Presumably, healthy human beings will respond similarly to a sudden blast of heat, regardless of culture, but only people from certain cultures will be able to interpret the warning label, the traffic signal, and the map. If we think of the heat response as part of the hardware in our systems, the cultural dimension is more like software. Yet if culture can be intelligibly interpreted to be like software, it is software that functions down to a very basic level— comparable to, say, the computer's Basic Input/Output System (BIOS), operating system, or software platform. The cultural orientations—like the BIOS, operating system, and platform—have to be introduced to the computer at the boot-up level before more complex programs are loaded onto it. Culture operates on a range of levels comparable to the computer's software that extends from the BIOS up to the most sophisticated programs.

Cultural structures are like computer software in another way as well. I generally expect my cultural orientation and computer software to be invisible in the conduct of everyday affairs, to be "user-friendly." I typically think about them only when encountering a dysfunction. In the case of the computer, I notice the operating system only when there is, for example, a conflict within a program that causes it to hang or when there is an inability to transfer information across software platforms. There are analogous times when I become acutely aware of my deeply embedded cultural patterns and processes. At such moments, either the set of rules for how to respond is for some reason suddenly inaccessible or two conflicting instructions arise simultaneously. Like the computer, I need a clear protocol or I am locked up in hesitation. Cultural training typically occurs when a child is under the guidance of elders or when one wants to learn to function less as an alien in a foreign milieu. The training aims to remove glitches that would cause conflicts in the most fundamental protocols (how to address different kinds of people, how to extend greetings, gratitude, and condolences, and so forth) or rules of harmonious interaction (whether to bear right or left in the face of oncomers, whether to form a queue while waiting, how to hail a taxi). As with any fundamental "programming," there is arbitrariness. Things could be—and indeed are—done differently in various cultures. Nature does not inform me whether to bear right or left in traffic. Yet culture (using repetition, habit, and routinization) creates a "second nature" enabling me to act "spontaneously" with others in predictable ways so that everyday life can proceed with as little hesitation as possible. This second nature often functions neurologically as conditioned responses—acquired behavioral habits that typically function immediately and without reflection. They are so ingrained as to be dependable and trustworthy.

On a still higher level of complexity, the difficulties of transferring information across different computer software platforms or even radically different programs within the same operating system (for example, transferring data from a relational to a hierarchical database program) is much like the problem of intercultural communication, especially translation. In fact, we even use the term "translate" to describe such a computer operation. I may often know what I want to communicate, but somehow it gets scrambled in the transfer to the other person's linguistic, cultural, or computer context. The frustrations between Macintosh and PC owners when such a transfer fails, for example, can bear an unsettling resemblance to breakdowns in intercultural communication. However cooperative each side might seem, they both secretly believe there is something irrational, defective, or unsophisticated about the other system. "Why can't a Mac think like an IBM (or vice versa)?" To the computer user— or to the member of a culture or subculture—one's own system seems the most "natural," "intuitive," and "easily understood." That is because it has become second nature through training and routinization.

These sophisticated problems of mutual unintelligibility and untranslatability bring to the fore a new complexity: reflection. Reflection recognizes that the results of one kind of processing (by a computer or by a culture) are not necessarily accessible to another mode of processing. For example, one program may not recognize links made by another program. Or the words and concepts of one culture may translate poorly, if at all, into another. The person who is competent in both programs or both cultures knows that for some tasks one alternative is more efficient than the other (and vice versa), although overall each works quite well. Translation across boundaries is more difficult in proportion to how much programmatic or cultural processing is involved. In the computer realm, for instance, it is relatively easy to translate the letters of ordinary text but hard to translate formatting and special fonts across platforms. Culturally, it is easier to translate a term like "sun" across unrelated languages than a word like "soul."

Applying the computer analogy to the next two chapters, we could say that when a culture's operating system foregrounds one orientation—intimacy or integrity—over the other, this preference profoundly influences how higher-order, more complex, programs can function in a society. Whether I should understand relations as primarily external or internal, for example, is a simple question. In all fairness, there are advantages and disadvantages to each and I can imagine making a choice in favor of either. In fact, I may even wonder why I must choose at all. Yet the question is so fundamental and the consequences so complex that it might be compared to choosing whether to use the Macintosh or the PC platform. Depending on my choice, I will have different options for sophisticated software programs and different procedures for using them.

We have seen that cultural systems tend to develop a second nature that allows its members to be consistent, predictable, and dependable. This applies as much to conceptual issues as to quotidian ones like whether to keep to the right or left in traffic. On the conceptual level, living together in society requires us to engage in common discourse: to analyze, argue, and persuade. People need to negotiate differences, to teach the next generation, to reflect on feelings and ideas and articulate them. Such communication requires ground rules for thought and expression. Of such higher-order cultural programs, there are those that deal primarily with what-is (epistemology, logical argument, and metaphysics) and those that deal primarily with what ought-to-be (aesthetics, ethics, and politics). These two kinds of philosophical enterprises are the focus of the next two chapters. As we proceed, the basic orientations of intimacy and integrity will continue to reiterate themselves into ever more complex configurations. Yet as we saw in the analysis of the two trees in the Introduction, no matter how complex the diagrams might become, the complexity derives from the reiteration of simple patterns.

# CHAPTER 4

# INTIMACY AND INTEGRITY
## AS WORLDVIEWS

*EPISTEMOLOGY, ANALYSIS AND ARGUMENT,*

*AND METAPHYSICS*

Table 1 summarizes the differences between the orientations of intimacy and integrity as we have discussed them thus far. Building on these differences between intimacy and integrity, we will examine what follows philosophically from making one orientation dominant over the other. As explained in chapter 3, the orientation of either intimacy and integrity establishes something like an "operating system" on which more complex "programs" of thought can run—essentially philosophical programs that determine how we tend to think about the world, ourselves, and society.

**Table 1. General Characteristics of Integrity and Intimacy**

| *Characteristic* | *Integrity* | *Intimacy* |
|---|---|---|
| Basis of verification | Objective and public | Objective and nonpublic ("expert") |
| Form of relationship | External (Figure 8) | Internal (Figure 9) |
| Affective component | No affect | Affectively charged |
| Somatic component (mimetic praxis) | Not emphasized | Emphasized |
| Reflective nature of its ground | Bright, clear | Dark |

In this chapter we will focus on ontology and the building of a worldview: the domains of epistemology, rational argument or analysis, and metaphysics. Let us begin with epistemology.

## EPISTEMOLOGY: INTEGRITY'S VERSION

What do we know and how do we know it? These are the fundamental questions behind epistemology, the philosophical study of knowledge. The knowing process itself, however, looks quite different depending on which orientation, intimacy or integrity, predominates. How, for example, are the knower and known related? In the integrity orientation, the person and the object (let us for now call this object "reality") are understood to exist separately; knowledge is the name for a kind of external connection between them (see Figure 15). In such an understanding of knowledge, the knower and the known maintain their respective integrity such that the reality is unchanged whether or not it is in relation with the knower. Conversely, the knower is intrinsically the same whether or not she or he is in relation to the known. This model has several important consequences.

First, as we have seen, the integrity-based model of knowing assumes a publicly verifiable objectivity. Through objective distance the knower is an observer of the real and does not let emotions or affect color either the known object or the relationship between knower and known. Given the knower's independence from the known, any other potential knower will (at least when situated correctly) be able to attain the same knowledge of reality. Because integrity's knowledge (the $R$ between the knower $a$ and known $b$) maintains $b$'s integrity, $a$'s knowledge of $b$ leaves $b$ unchanged

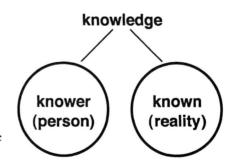

FIGURE 15. Knowledge as External Relation

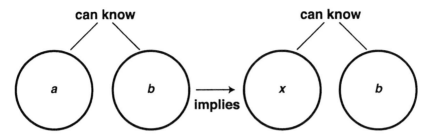

FIGURE 16. From One Knower to All Knowers

for another knower to enter into the same knowing relation with *b*. The knower is theoretically interchangeable with any other knower in such an integrity orientation. In effect: if *a* knows *b* and *R* represents *a*'s knowing relation to *b*, then *aRb* is such that *a* becomes merely a particular value for a general variable *x*. That is: if *a* knows *b*, then *x* as well can know *b*, assuming *x* is anyone with rational capacity and relevant information. Diagrammatically we get Figure 16, where *a* is a particular knowing person, *b* is the known reality, and *x* is any person with a capacity to know. In an integrity-based epistemology there is an agreed upon set of rules and principles to guide the knower. These rules may be conscious or unconscious. But even in the latter case, one could reflectively go back and unearth the formerly unconscious principles. In our terminology we say the principles can be "brought to light." This process is the basis for settling disagreements over what is known. To know entails accord with the principles of knowing that apply universally to all cases and persons. This approach assures that knowledge is not only objective but also public.

Second, an integrity-based model of knowing generally supports a correspondence theory of truth. That is: truth occurs when there is a correspondence between the ideas in the knower and the reality existing separately from the knower. Such a correspondence is an external relation between knower and reality because two different items (an idea and reality) are related in a special way (the correspondence). This relationship has implications for how the integrity orientation construes the knowledge of discovery, for example. In its orientation, we assume first that reality preexists the idea, then the idea is developed, and finally a relationship between the two is tested by the approved rules of verification. If this external relation turns out to be one of correspondence, we have

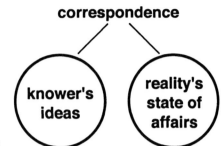

**FIGURE 17.** Integrity's
Knowledge as Correspondence

knowledge. In Galileo's discovery of Jupiter's satellites, for instance, there are three stages. Long before Galileo was born, Jupiter had its moons (stage one). Then Galileo saw in his telescope specks of light that seemed to move about the planet (stage two). Surmising they might be moons, Galileo studied the movements in terms of the mathematics of orbits, confirming the hypothesized relationship between his ideas and the reality out in space (stage three). Here we have the three parts of an external relation as developed sequentially: the preexistent reality *(b)*, the hypothesizing idea *(a)*, and the verifiability test between them that establishes the knowing relationship *(R)*. See Figure 17.

A third characteristic of an integrity-based epistemology relates to language's ability to express truth. Although natural language can be used in a variety of ways, an integrity-grounded epistemology generally designates one use as distinctively relevant—namely, the referential mode. In fact, for many epistemologists operating in the integrity orientation, this is the only use of language that can function as the proper relationship between knower and known. In assuming that knowledge does not impinge on the integrity of either the knower or the known, one common form of epistemology (epitomized by logical positivism) assumes that knowledge resembles a prism that refracts through the senses the things and relations within reality into the words and syntactic relations within language. In this way, knowledge—as formulated within language—pictures reality in some way. The statement "John walks the dog" is true, for example, if and only if the word "John" designates an independently existing thing, the phrase "the dog" does the same, and the function designated by the word "walks" applies to the relation between these two things. In other words: the sentence has two nouns that are related by a verb in a way analogous to the two things being related by the activity. If

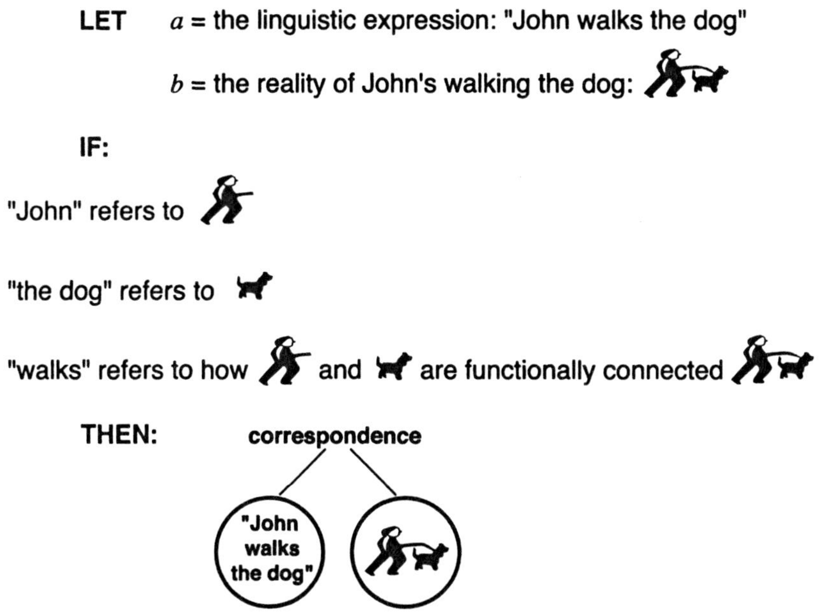

LET    $a$ = the linguistic expression: "John walks the dog"

b = the reality of John's walking the dog:

IF:

"John" refers to

"the dog" refers to

"walks" refers to how     and     are functionally connected

THEN:        correspondence

"John walks the dog"

FIGURE 18. Language as Correspondence

the relation among the words "corresponds" to the relations among the things, the statement must be true. Figure 18 expresses this situation diagrammatically.

A spin-off of this view of language is important to many forms of integrity-oriented epistemologies—namely, what corresponds to the reality relation is not necessarily in the natural language of the knower. In mirroring reality, according to this view, language is itself referring to a structure purporting to be about the way things are. So language does not directly picture reality; rather, language denotes a conceptual relation that is then compared to reality. Following this line of analysis, statements in different languages depicting the same state of affairs are understood to be asserting the same thing. *"Fritz ist ein Deutscher"* asserts exactly the same thing as "Fritz is a German." What is asserted—that which is independent of the natural language in which it is expressed—is the proposition. Formal logic can then analyze the possible and necessary connections among various propositions by using a notation that is independent of any particular natural language. In doing so, formal logic is as unconfined by any natural language of human beings as is a mathematical

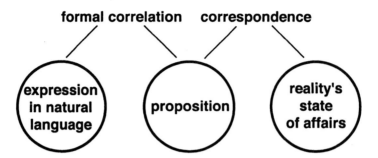

FIGURE 19. Language to Proposition to Reality

statement in the notation "1 + 2 = 3." The pronunciation of this mathematical statement may differ from country to country, but as a symbolic statement it is readily understood by most people in the world. Figure 19 illustrates this relational situation.

That the propositional theory leads to a formal logic is understandable when we consider the relation between person and language to be external. Epistemologically this means that a statement, once it is properly stated in propositional form, is true or false independently of who says it or in what language it was originally uttered. It has, as it were, its own integrity as a claim to truth. Furthermore, within such an integrity orientation the proposition designates only the "state of affairs" and tells us nothing about the affect of the speaker. Because the integrity orientation considers the affective component to be fundamentally irrelevant to knowledge, the loss of affect is considered to be no epistemological loss at all. Indeed, if one is to be "objective" in integrity's terms, the affect must be neutralized or at least bracketed out of consideration. As symbolic logic developed into an ersatz language with its own syntax, it was a small step to make this into the "language" of computers. This development has had great value, especially in areas requiring sophisticated computation. Yet it is also clear that a computer does not ordinarily duplicate the ways human beings learn or reason out decisions. Therefore, a more recent agenda for applying the correspondence theory of truth has been in the field of artificial intelligence. This enterprise attempts to make the computer's functions "correspond" to the patterns of human thought so that the computer can represent and predict human decision making. In short: for some integrity-based epistemologies at least, the field has shifted from describing the world as existing independently of the human mind to describing operations of the mind itself.

## EPISTEMOLOGY: INTIMACY'S VERSION

Now let us contrast this way of knowing with an epistemology arising from the assumption that knower and known are in an orientation of intimacy rather than integrity. In this case the person and the reality are in an internal, not external, relation. That is: knower and known are not fully discrete; they overlap in some way and part of this overlap is knowledge. The knowledge is still a relation between the person and reality, but this relation is part of the knower and known, not an external bond connecting them. If we think about knowledge in terms of discovery, in this model the discovery is about the knower as well as the known. When we learn something intimately, we learn, in part, about ourselves. To view knowledge in this light is radically different from the integrity orientation in which knowledge is an external relation between the person and the world. Let us examine some of the epistemological consequences of this intimacy-based model of knowledge. See Figure 20.

Earlier we noted that the intimacy orientation tends to view knowledge as objective without being public. When we understand knowledge to be in the overlap of knower and known, it is clear why it cannot be public: to access the knowledge fully, we must also access (be at least partly "inside") the knower. Let us return to one of our earlier examples: the Olympic judges' intimate knowledge of the sport of diving. The judges' objective perception of subtle differences in the quality of style is not a knowledge that can be tested by just anyone. It derives from the judges' expertise developed over years of participation in the sport—first as athlete perhaps, then coach, then judge. Only judges who have gone through a similar experience can know the basis of the judgment. That is: the evaluation of style occurs in the overlap between the judge and the sport. Those who have never taken part in the sport or thought of the sport as part of themselves have no objective basis for such expert

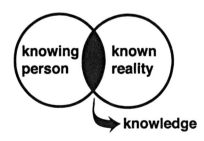

FIGURE 20. Intimacy Between Knower and Known

judgments. There is a related point, mentioned earlier, that is worth examining more closely. The expert knowledge of the judge is objective—objective in the sense that other judges who are similarly part of the sport will be in remarkable agreement with each other in the scoring of style. Yet, unlike the objective knowledge born of integrity relationships, the acquisition of this knowledge does not come from detached, dispassionate observation of the sport. Because it involves a lifetime of participation, we might even say it is an objectivity born of love for the sport. As we recall, love is an internal relationship of the intimacy sort and it is out of this love that part of the sport becomes the judge and the judge part of the sport. It is similar to the way loving parents get to know their children or even caring teachers their students.

Earlier we noted that the epistemologies born of the integrity model of relationship tend to favor correspondence theories of truth. What about the intimacy-based epistemologies? No mainstream modern Western theory of truth is a neat fit. Since the correspondence theory is generally taken to assume some distance between the person who knows and the reality that is known, it is not appropriate. In the intimacy model, part of the person is the reality and part of the reality is the person. An overlap implies an identification rather than correspondence. A coherence theory of truth, by contrast, typically suggests conceptual links such as the axioms, postulates, and theorems in a geometric system. Yet because intimate knowledge is achieved through a praxis that allows the knower to overlap with the known, it is, as we saw in chapter 2, somatic as much as intellectual. The basis of the intimate knowledge is "dark," and its foundation cannot be "brought to light" in an axiomatic manner. Thus neither the coherence nor the correspondence theory readily suits the kind of truth we find in the intimacy orientation.

What about the pragmatic theory of truth? In some ways, it is the most intriguing candidate for explaining the kind of intimate knowledge we are exploring. In the pragmatic theory, truth lies in whether the proposed knowledge works. In such a pragmatic view, there is both a connection to praxis and an involvement of the personal (including possibly an affective) dimension—two points suggestive of the kind of intimate knowledge we are discussing here. Yet the pragmatic theory often allows for a private truth: "It works for me." (William James seemed to speak this way in applying pragmatism to belief in his *Will to Believe,* for example.) The intimate knowledge with which we are dealing, however, requires a greater objectivity. The Olympic judges as a group are expected to agree, just as religious people with a common praxis are typically expected to agree about what is known through faith. Furthermore, the agreement among the Olympic judges is not reached by consensus, compromise, or discussion. Each judge independently comes up with a score nearly identical to those of the other judges. This explains the objective, though not public, character of the knowledge. Expert knowledge can only be, and is expected to be, tested by other experts. In a craft or in a religious tradition that has masters and apprentices, only a master can certify the skill or insight of a disciple and only an established master can certify a new master.

Perhaps we need to coin a new term capturing the theory of truth involved in an intimacy orientation. In this book we will call it the "assimilation theory of truth." The term "assimilation" captures the sense that both the knower and the known overlap in some way. It implies that the potential knower comes into the situation with an openness to the other —a readiness to be transformed. At the same time the potential object of the knowledge is taken to be not completely fixed. The known in an intimacy orientation is not simply a fixed given; rather, it seems to be an offering of itself to the intimacy of knowledge. The term "assimilation" is used in physiology to indicate the process by which the body takes in nutrients from the food that has been ingested and digested. This usage is suggestive of the somatic dimension of intimacy. From the standpoint of intimacy, knowledge is absorbed into the body somatically through praxis. Knowledge is literally incorporated rather than received from outside or generated from inside. When we refer to something difficult to understand or know as being "hard to digest," we are using the rhetoric of intimacy's epistemology. Similarly the archaic use of "to know" someone— meaning "to be sexually intimate with" that person—captures as well the somatic aspect of sharing.

How, then, can a claim to knowledge be verified in intimacy's forms of epistemology? In an important sense, intimate knowledge is not something the person has. Instead it is what that person, at least in part, is. (In Sanskrit, *"satya"* means both "being" and "truth.") Knowledge is assimilated, not acquired. It resides in the overlap between the knower and the known. Therefore, the claim to knowledge can be judged only by someone who already knows the object intimately and has some insight into the claimant as well. Insofar as this judge knows the object intimately, he or she can recognize someone else's having that knowledge. Such a test is possible for two reasons. First, the judge and the candidate for knowledge must have undergone a similar praxis that has allowed them to assimilate the knowledge. This praxis has given both the judge and the candidate a common experience from which the judge can make an evaluation. Second, assuming that the candidate has been an apprentice to some master of the knowledge (in fact the judge might have been the candidate's mentor), we find the knowledge embedded not just in a single individual but in a community as well. The community is one of shared praxis and personal conjunction such that its members know each other as well as the "object" of the knowledge. From the community's involvement in its common praxis and its fruits, it can judge the extent of assimilation within the professed knower. Indeed, the examiner (the master) must himself or herself be deemed an expert by the community of experts. Many esoteric communities, medieval guilds, and artistic schools of performance typify such criteria and procedures.

To sum up this point about the test of intimate knowledge: the master can evaluate the apprentice's knowledge only by knowing both the apprentice and the reality. Figure 21 depicts the situation. The master $(m)$ has a nearly complete intimate knowledge $(K)$ of the reality $(r)$ in question (note that the diagram shows a very large overlap between the two) and the apprentice $(a)$ has a significant knowledge $(K')$ of $(r)$ as well (but not as much as the master). The master, through the shared praxis and also via knowledge of the community of praxis and its sense of the apprentice's progress, knows the apprentice quite well. The test of the apprentice's qualifications to become a new master is, therefore, in the conjunction $(K'')$ of the master, apprentice, and reality. From this standpoint, the master can determine the extent and depth of the intimacy between the apprentice and the reality. This determination, in turn, reflects the master's own internal knowledge with the reality.

Let us consider further this issue of the overlap, the internal relation, between knower and known. The implication is that the knower is affect-

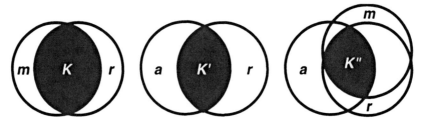

FIGURE 21. Testing Intimate Knowledge

ed by the known and the known by the knower. If we have been acculturated in an integrity orientation, this seems a bit odd. The first half of the claim—the influence of the known on the knower—is perhaps more familiar. Because of what we already know, we learn about certain things in a certain way. Our knowledge is cumulative: what we have learned forms the basis for further knowledge. In this sense, at least, the process of knowing changes the knower. The other half of the relation—how the knower transforms the known—may not be so obvious to those steeped in the integrity orientation. For intimacy, the known world is not what it would be without its knowers. From such an orientation, human knowledge is not merely the hunting and gathering of information; it is the mutual transformation of both world and human being.

The change in the known is most obvious when we consider artistic or technological transformation. Those steeped in integrity's forms of knowing are also engaged in artistic and technological transformation of the world, of course, but here we are discussing something different about the emergence and nature of these human transformations. As we saw in chapter 1's example of Michelangelo seeing "David" in the uncarved block of marble, the statue *David* could not be what it is without the intersection between the block of marble and Michelangelo's artistic skill or sensitivity. Michelangelo's knowledge of "David" and the emergence of *David* through the artist's hands are not fully separable acts. Let us try a more pedestrian example. As I sit in a coffee shop writing this, I can look around and wonder what is *not* the interplay between human knowledge and world. The building, the furniture, the electrical equipment, the lights, the clothing I wear—these are the realities I now experience. Surely I see the plants and trees out the window, but they are part of the planned landscaping for the building's grounds. I experience them not just as articles of reality but also as artifices and artifacts of human activity.

Someone might object: "But those things are not *my* artifices or artifacts. They are just givens out there in the world I encounter and are intrinsically no different from the trees of a forest or the clouds in the sky." This is integrity talking: the person is being conceived as intrinsically separate from the external world and separate from other human beings, at least until an external relationship of some kind takes form. Suppose instead we see the person as not only overlapping with the world but with other people as well. Then, through my being in this coffeehouse, I am connected not only with the world but also with the architects and builders who made the building. The coffee shop itself exists as the real-ization of the owner's dream or idea. Indeed, the founders' picture is on the wall and by sharing in the ambience of the shop, I am sharing something with them. Such an intimate way of thinking about architectural structures may help us understand the cathedrals of Europe, which often took centuries to construct. As it was being built, a cathedral held the attention and dedication of the generations of guildsmen who constructed it—even though most of them would never live to see the final product. For them, perhaps, the building was part of themselves, as they were part of the building. The building would be used by centuries of faithful religious devotees and perhaps in creating that sacred space the guildsmen felt internally connected with the tradition that would someday exist and the merits of spirituality thriving therein. Of course, no one can prove empirically that there exists such an internal relationship among workers, the devout, and the building. There can be no public verification of such intimacy. But in seeing myself as a builder and creator, I may have an intuition about how others may have felt.

Furthermore, as noted in our discussion of the intimacy between a person and that person's "personal effects" in chapter 2, I am not isolated in this coffeehouse. There are regular customers who are here almost every morning. We know each other's favorite chairs and basic habits. As I enter the door in the morning, a staff member gets my mug ready to pour my cup of coffee. If something should happen and one of the regulars stopped coming, we would feel the coffeehouse is somehow transformed. All the regulars would feel odd (therein is the "objectivity") if some stranger came in and took the absentee's chair. The regulars' intimate knowledge of the coffeehouse and its internal relations transforms the meaning of the reality as experienced by the insiders. In short: insofar as I establish an intimate way of knowing the coffee shop, something that happens only as I become part of it, the shop itself changes.

The integrity-oriented critic might grant that insofar as the world is modified by humanity, we can say human knowledge has transformed its object. (Of course, an integrity form of knowing may also transform the world. But the way in which it does so is normatively different, as we will see in the next chapter's discussion of aesthetics and ethics.) What if instead of being in a coffee shop, however, I were in a more natural setting—taking a walk across the snow in a forest, for example? There is no communal construction in the forest with which I overlap (discounting the trails blazed by predecessors). There is just the world "out there" and me "over here." The integrity of both is clear and inviolable. At least, this is how an integrity orientation might lead us to think about the situation. If we foreground intimacy instead of integrity, however, our take of the situation will change. Now language begins to be particularly relevant. As I walk through the forest, learning about its nature, I use concepts that are not strictly mine and words for these concepts that are almost certainly never strictly my own. Indeed, there is reality out there and I am knowing it. But the known reality out there is shaped by how the "out there" has taught me to know it. "Out there" includes the concepts learned in biology class and the language learned as a child. I do not simply perceive a world; I perceive a learned gestalt of the world. This gestalt has become incorporated into my second nature and is as much a part of my knowledgeable perception as the scents stimulating my olfactory nerves. If I were now to be trained as a Native American medicine man, I might assimilate the forest through a very different gestalt. The world around me would no longer be a nature trail waiting for botanical labels but an apothecary waiting for medical identification and use in therapy. The known is altered by the knower. The meaning of the forest—indeed what it *can* possibly mean—is inseparable from its use. In short: in the overlap between knower and known, we also find the structures of a socially acquired language. From the standpoint of an intimacy-dominant epistemology, knowledge occurs in the conjunction of self, reality, and community.

Such an analysis suggests that, for intimacy, language is part of the world-as-experienced. The intimacy orientation understands language to be in the overlap of self and world. It is at once part of me and part of the world I perceive, analyze, and articulate. As we will see in the next chapter, this has implications for aesthetics. For epistemology, the relevance is that within a context of intimacy the knower recognizes that one's concepts and words were acquired through communal praxis. Guided by masters, mentors, and elders, praxis teaches what is important. It is not surprising, therefore, that many words learned through the praxis are not shared by those outside it. The community of shared praxis often has a technical vocabulary intimating the subtleties of the knowledge unknown to those not so sensitized. The proper use of such vocabulary identifies one as a part of a community of knowers. This foregrounds the idea that knowledge is communal and represents the result of a specific praxis. In the intimacy orientation, knowledge is not expressed as something universal (as we saw in integrity's emphasis on universals and

symbolic logic) but as intimations for a special audience: those who share
in the praxis yielding the expert knowledge.

## RATIONAL ARGUMENT AND ANALYSIS:
## THE MEANING OF CONTRADICTION

First I need to explain what I mean by "rational argument and analysis."
For my purposes, we can think of a rational argument or mode of rational analysis as a culturally approved form of persuasion or way of systematic investigation that conforms, on the one hand, to a few basic rules of
intelligibility (such as the law of noncontradiction described in chapter 1)
and, on the other, to the appropriate cultural orientation such as integrity
or intimacy. Within a cultural context, rational argument is the endorsed
form of reasoning allowing us to articulate what follows from what is
known or assumed to be true. It is a way of understanding the necessary
and contingent connections among ideas, statements, or positions and a
way of establishing the hierarchy of values. This way of posing the issue
sidesteps some of the confusion around the idea of culture and logic discussed in chapter 1. Our present definition allows us to agree that there
may be major differences among cultures or subcultures in their forms of
rational argument without assuming any violation of the basic principles
necessary to a conception of intelligibility: the law of noncontradiction,
for example. Because the discussion of this issue has historically been such
a muddle, it may be worthwhile to expand a bit further on how neither
integrity's emphasis on external relations nor intimacy's emphasis on internal relations is necessarily in violation of the law of noncontradiction.

   If we simply apply the diagrams for external and internal relations (Figures 8 and 9), we can see a source for much of the confusion in this area.
From within the integrity orientation, we might depict the relation between $a$ and its opposite not-$a$ $(\sim\!a)$ as either Figure 22$a$ or 22$b$. (The latter is more common.) The point of either diagram is that $a$ is not in any
way $\sim\!a$ and vice versa. This is a clear and tight distinction. But it may
seem to run counter to common ways of thinking insofar as we sometimes meaningfully assert things like "it is green and it isn't" or "she's
both smart and not smart." So it is advisable to add the Aristotelian
qualifier—namely, that logically something cannot be both $a$ and $\sim\!a$ in
exactly the same way at exactly the same time. This affirms the intelligi-

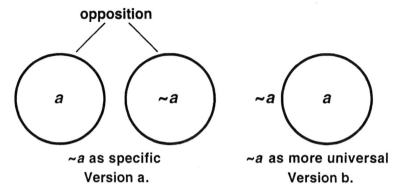

FIGURE 22. Contradiction as External Relation

bility of these common expressions by pointing out their elliptical character. In "it is green and it isn't," for example, we may actually mean something like "it is green in one sense, but not green in another." That is: it may be green in the sense that is within the spectrum's range of wavelengths we commonly call "green," but it is not fully green because it also has tiny speckles of dark blue or because it appears green under certain lighting conditions but not others (like an iridescent piece of cloth, for example). And in saying "she's both smart and not smart" we may mean "she is smart in some circumstances (for example, in handling finances) but not in others (for example, in judging character)." These interpretations of ordinary kinds of speaking preserve integrity's take on the law of noncontradiction. This is rather straightforward in the case of external relations as posed in the integrity orientation. But when we turn to intimacy's emphasis on internal relations, its defense against being a violation of the law of noncontradiction may not be so obvious.

What is intimacy's take on the law of noncontradiction? Our first inclination might be to say the relation between *a* and *~a* can be represented as in Figure 23. This is initially confusing. It seems odd to claim that

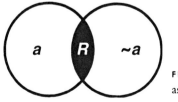

FIGURE 23. Contradiction
as Internal Relation

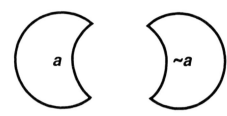

FIGURE 24. Contradiction
as Broken Intimacy?

opposites actually overlap somehow—that what is $R$ is somehow both $a$
and $\sim a$. The first point to bear in mind is that intimacy avoids thinking of
things, even conceptual things, as self-enclosed, indivisible units ("integers"). For intimacy, therefore, "$a$ is $\sim a$" does not entail that $a$ and $\sim a$
have absolutely *nothing* in common—that they are self-contained units
whose identities are inviolate. If we were to think of only the *part* of $a$
that does not overlap the *part* of $\sim a$, we would have no violation of the
law of noncontradiction. That is: in what is outside the relation $R$, we
would have only the "broken intimacy" model we used earlier (as we see
in Figure 24). Here we find no overlap, so noncontradiction is preserved.

If only it were that simple. In saving noncontradiction, Figure 24 sup-
presses interdependence. Sometimes thinkers in an intimacy orientation
are so insistent on the importance of interdependence that one may assert
"$a$ can only be fully $a$ insofar as it is in some way interdependent with $\sim a$
and vice versa." That is: while intimacy can accept the accuracy of Figure
24, this depiction does not capture what it finds most important. Something is missing in these representations—namely, the interdependence
between $a$ and $\sim a$. From this perspective, we save the principle of noncontradiction only by relinquishing the kind of internal relatedness distinctive to intimacy. Let us return to our everyday expression that something may be "green and not green." We can represent this as Figure 25.

In Figure 25 the $R$ can mean something like "ways of being thought

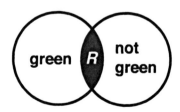

FIGURE 25. Internal Relation
Between Green and Not Green

of in terms of the category 'green.'" For the sake of streamlining our language, I will henceforth use the word "greenness" to refer to this $R$. But in doing so, I am not assuming anything necessarily metaphysical in using this word. For us to make the judgment either that "it is green" or "it is not green," we assume that *both* of these statements are about greenness in some way. To claim that something is green or not green is to assert there is a relationship between this something and greenness. In short: it is not a "category mistake" to apply the concept of greenness to this something.

When philosophers talk of a category mistake, they mean the category being considered is not appropriate to the thing to which it is being applied. It makes sense, for example, to ask "is this leaf green or not green?" But it does not make sense to ask "is height green or not green?" To say "height is not green" is in one sense true but in another misleading. Height is not green because it is not any color at all. This is different from saying the rose blossom is not green because it is red. Because color is a characteristic of rose blossoms, it is appropriate (not a category mistake) to inquire about its greenness and to conclude it is "not green." Returning to our diagrams, in Figure 25 the $R$ represents the "greenness" and its overlap with both $a$ and $\sim a$ assures us that no category mistake is involved in asking whether it is green. It follows, then, that every time we truthfully assert something is green, we are also affirming something in common with a false assertion that it is not green—namely, that greenness is appropriate when talking about such a thing as the one in question. Such appropriateness is not highlighted in integrity's depiction of noncontradiction in Figure 22*b,* for example. More precisely, in using the formal logical notation of *"a"* and *"~a,"* Figure 22*b* may be assuming, but not explicitly showing, that there is no category mistake. In this diagram, both "the leaf that is not green" and "height that is not green" would fall into the area designated by $\sim a$. Thus, as we might expect from our analysis of cultural orientations, it is not so much that integrity and intimacy disagree over the nature of noncontradiction. Instead they foreground different aspects as crucial for their respective purposes. Integrity emphasizes the radical separateness of $a$ and $\sim a$; intimacy emphasizes the inseparability within their differentiation.

How do we account for these two different takes on the law of noncontradiction? The law itself actually says less than either Figures 22 *(a* or *b)* or Figure 23 suggests. Minimally conceived, the law of noncontradic-

FIGURE 26. Minimal Representation of the Law
of Noncontradiction

tion (something cannot be both fully *a* and fully ~*a* in exactly the same
way at exactly the same time) could be construed as saying no more than
Figure 26. Both intimacy and integrity could accept this characterization
of the law. Because of their respective ways of construing meaning, however, they necessarily enhance this minimalist interpretation in a way most
suitable to each of their purposes.

Although my discussion may lack the precision of formal logic, it is
enough to suggest how arguments are commonly articulated in the two
orientations. In fact, my definition of "rational" or "rational analysis" is
intentionally broad enough to include some of the domain of what is
often called "rhetoric"—that is, the forms of discourse used to argue or
persuade. We are primarily explaining the approved rules for analysis, understanding, and rational persuasion in these two cultural orientations.
This suggests that the issue is really about what is culturally authoritative
in a form of argument. This claim does not assert there are no common
logical laws shared by different cultural orientations. We can, I have argued, maintain the universality of a few laws of logic (necessary for basic
intelligibility) while also accepting that different cultures or subcultures
may have a different take on what is most crucial in such laws—perhaps
in the end even leading to a distinctive formal logical system. Such a different system would presumably be helpful in analyzing topics ignored or
poorly handled in a different formal system.

It is vital, too, to distinguish this sense of rational argument or analysis from ontology or metaphysics. The analysis of authoritative rhetorics
explicates how we communicate, persuade, and convince, not how reality
itself may or may not be. As we will see, a certain rational way of analyzing might suggest or even presume that reality is one way or another. But
it neither establishes that this is the case nor requires that it be so. A

philosopher may even claim that the relation among concepts in an analysis must be fundamentally different from how things are actually related. The Indian Buddhist philosopher Nāgārjuna argued this point explicitly almost two millennia ago in his *Mūlamadhyamāka Kārikā*. Much later in the West, Kant argued more modestly that the categories operative in knowing cannot be shown to reflect the way reality is in itself. Aristotle's criticism of Plato's theory of the forms pointed out the danger in making too quick a leap from rational analysis to ontology. Specifically, Aristotle argued that merely because analysis can distinguish form from matter does not imply (as Plato seems to have believed) that form and matter exist separately from each other. What is analytically distinguishable, Aristotle insisted, is not necessarily ontologically distinct. The contrast between rational analysis and ontology will be important not only in the final sections of this chapter but also in the conclusions developed in chapter 6. For now, however, let us consider how the orientations of integrity and intimacy influence the approved paradigms of rational argument.

## RATIONAL ARGUMENT AND ANALYSIS: INTEGRITY'S WHOLE-AS-PARTS AND USE OF BIPOLARITY

If a culture or subculture emphasizes the integrity orientation, what paradigms of rational argument and analysis might emerge as most important? Here we will consider two: the modes of reasoning utilizing the paradigm of the whole-as-parts and the paradigm of bipolarity. Let us begin with the whole-as-parts. Within integrity-defined relationships it makes sense to understand the whole in terms of the parts constituting it. That is: the whole consists only of all its parts and the ways they relate. Using this paradigm, the analysis of any object $x$ involves identifying parts of the whole and determining how these parts are connected to each other. Thus one might try to understand the political state in terms of individuals who have entered into an external relationship; language in terms of sentences or words tied together in some way; nature in terms of its flora, fauna, weather, topography, geology, and their connections; ethics in terms of individuals related through rights and responsibilities; experience in terms of objects, sensations, perceptions, and the interpretations

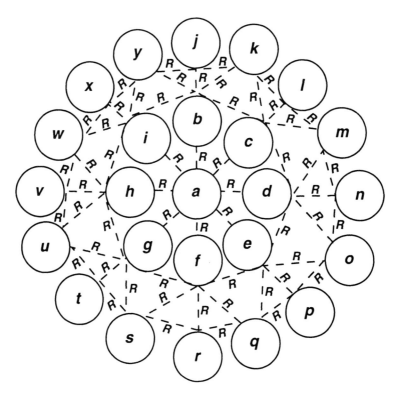

FIGURE 27. Integrity's Whole-as-Parts Paradigm

connecting them. Diagramatically we can represent this paradigm of analysis as Figure 27.

It is easy to see how this whole-as-parts paradigm displays its roots in the integrity orientation. If the whole has its own integrity, it is an indivisible whole not open to further analysis. If the whole can be analyzed, it can be broken down into the smallest units having integrity. These units are then the building blocks of the whole and the only question for further analysis is how these integrity units, the parts, are externally related to each other. This leads to a view of rational analysis having two steps. First we identify the essential qualities of individual, indivisible entities. Then we analyze the relations among these indivisible entities. In short: the discrete parts plus their external relations constitute the whole. In Figure 27 the whole is broken down into its smallest, individual units $(a–y)$ and all their external relationships $(R)$—which, of course, may be a range of external relations $R_1$, $R_2$, and so on.

The second paradigm emerging from the integrity orientation's primary mode of rational argument and analysis is bipolarity. Bipolarity structures rational thought in two ways. First, in trying to understand $x$ we may think of it as opposed to its opposite (or at least something very different against which it is contrasted). To understand light, for example, one might distinguish it from dark. Similarly, there are binaries of good/evil, rich/poor, freedom/oppression, and so forth. In trying to understand my own experience, I may analyze it in terms of a context defined by what-I-am vis-á-vis what-I-am-not. In this mode of analysis knowledge is defined in terms of I/it; individual ethics in terms of I/you or self/other; social ethics in terms of we/them; politics in terms of individual/state; gender studies in terms of masculine/feminine.

The other way the bipolarity paradigm might work is in defining or understanding something as *between* two opposites. Aristotle's golden mean for ethics functions in essentially this way. According to Aristotle, the virtue of courage, for example, is defined as what lies in the middle between the two polarities of foolhardiness and cowardice. In this case two options define the endpoints of a spectrum. (Their external relation is one of complete exclusion or opposition.) The third item, the focus of the analysis, is then defined in its external relationship to each of the poles. This allows the analysis that $x$ is on the spectrum going from pole $y$ to its binary opposite pole $z$ but might be "closer to" one of the two poles. When we find Aristotle's golden mean between the two extremes, the ethical option $e$ is such that the "distance" between one extreme $a$ and $e$ is equal to that between $e$ and the opposite extreme $\sim a$. In diagrammatic form we get Figure 28, where the relationship "degree of resemblance" $(R)$ is such that $R_1$ is equal to $R_2$.

Like the whole-as-parts paradigm, the bipolarity paradigm derives from the basic form of integrity relationships. Insofar as analysis is based

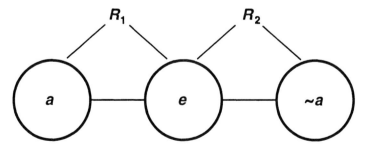

FIGURE 28. The Golden Mean

on sorting out the units of integrity and understanding their external relations, bipolarity may begin its analysis from the nature of the indivisible integrity units or from the external relation itself. Exemplifying the first possibility, suppose a member of an integrity-dominant culture or subculture is analyzing her own theistic experience. The poles of the analysis (also used in persuading someone about the rightness of theism) might be "self" and "what-self-is-not" (or the "wholly other")—namely, God. In analyzing such an experience one can analyze the relation between the two—namely, "faith." In this approach, faith is understood as an external relation (perhaps a contract or covenant) established between self and God. That is: the analysis starts from the nature of the relatents— examining the nature of God and self—and proceeds to articulating the kind of relationship that can connect them (faith). In some cases, in fact, this connection of contract or covenant may even be seen as a historical event connecting God and humankind in a special way. We might call this kind of analysis within the integrity orientation "ontological" insofar as it starts with an analysis of entities that exist and then discovers or hypothesizes relationships among them—perhaps relations that were established historically as in a creation narrative. Within the integrity orientation, the faith situation could also be analyzed in the opposite direction as well— that is, starting from an analysis of the relational experience of faith and proceeding to analyzing the two polarities connected by that relational experience. We might think of this approach as "phenomenological" instead of ontological insofar as it begins with the experiential and then isolates the bipolarities between which the experience was constituted (what Husserl called the "noesis" and "noema," for example). In the Western Christian tradition, early modern philosophy (of Descartes and Spinoza, say) commonly used such an ontological analysis. In the twentieth century, especially among the existential theologians (such as Paul Tillich in his *Dynamics of Faith*), the phenomenological analysis is often more prevalent. The point, though, is that despite their differences both the ontological and phenomenological analysis of faith can operate within an integrity orientation.

Before turning to the discussion of the analytic and argumentative paradigms arising from intimacy orientations, let us make one further observation about the logic of whole-as-parts and the logic of bipolarity. When we merge these two rational paradigms of integrity relationships, we have what we might call an "analysis via the individual." Such an individual may involve either a human or nonhuman element. We begin with the former. When we discuss a human phenomenon, the bipolar paradigm tends to frame the analysis in terms of a relation with the oppositional form "$h$ as contrasted with $n$" or "$h_1$ as contrasted with $h_2$," where $h$ stands for a human element in the interpretation and $n$ for a nonhuman element. In either case the two related elements are considered to be oppositional but connected by some external relation $R$. The human elements might be an individual person, an institution, or even humanity at large. Therefore an $h_1 R h_2$ relation could be I/you, self/society, self/other, or nation/world and $hRn$ relations could be I/it, humanity/nature, self/world, or society/environment. When this relation is further submitted to the whole-as-parts paradigm of argument and analysis, whenever the human element $h_x$ is something larger than an integerlike individual this element can be analyzed further into its component parts, ultimately down to the individual person. The "society" of the society/environment relation, for example, can be broken down further into individuals who collectively relate to each other externally as a (contractual) society. Therefore, an integrity argument may claim that the moral responsibility for preserving the integrity of the environment may rest ultimately in each individual person ("think globally, act locally"). In the next chapter we will see how this is an instance of a broad ethical paradigm, but here we are focusing only on the form of analysis or argument. Diagrammatically we get something like Figure 29, in which the analysis proceeds from the wholes to

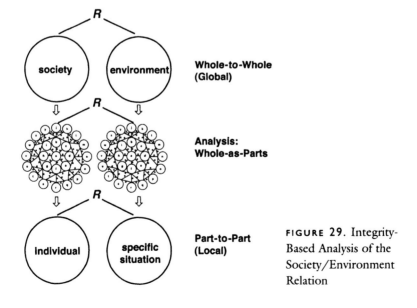

FIGURE 29. Integrity-Based Analysis of the Society/Environment Relation

the parts to the relation between part of society (the individual) to a part of the environment (the specific environmental situation). Through such an analysis, the society/environment relation can come down to the specifics of how I individually decide whether to use a plastic or biodegradable paper cup.

In treating two nonhuman phenomena ($n_1$ and $n_2$ standing for, say, flora and fauna), the two steps of the reasoning process are basically the same. Formulaically we have $n_1$ externally related to $n_2$. If, for instance, we start by trying to analyze $n_1$, we will do so in terms of its constituent parts and their external relations. To be thorough, we must then break down this $n_1$ into the parts constituting it as a whole until we reach the smallest individual entity for analysis: the indivisible entity with perfect integrity. Say, for example, that I am analyzing what has to be related for there to be a steel rod. I can describe it in terms of its chemical elements and their relationships with each other. But I can break this down further to the molecular, then atomic, and then subatomic units. In this manner the analysis proceeds from the relation between, for instance, iron and carbon to the relations among the subatomic particles. By the rationale of this form of analysis, I only understand something fully once I have reduced it to units that cannot be broken down further. It is not surprising that such an analysis yields a diagram resembling Figure 27: it is an "atomistic" mode of analysis. Furthermore, when analysis or argument combines the whole-as-parts paradigm with the bipolarity paradigm, it sometimes starts with an opposition between two nonhuman things ($n_1$ and $n_2$) but then continues to such a micro-level that the two opposing things are understood to be of the same kind. The opposition between matter and energy, for example, breaks down as the analysis moves to ever smaller units that are the building blocks of either or both. Such an analysis does not end in an overlap of matter and energy (as we might expect in the intimacy-dominant orientation). It results instead in a *unity* behind their difference.

The point of this admittedly abstract discussion is to reveal the underlying paradigms in the rational analyses and arguments arising from the orientation of integrity. When we step back far enough from the concrete specifics, we see that the form of analysis or argument is virtually the same when an environmental ethicist argues that pollution is *my* responsibility, when the physicist searches for the smallest micro-particle, when the geneticist in the Human Genome Project seeks the blueprint of human life, and so forth. That is: the ethicist places ultimate responsibility on the smallest unit of ethical integrity (the individual agent); the physicist breaks down the universe into its smallest indivisible units and their relations; the geneticist looks for the connections between the smallest genetic unit, the genes, and their relations to each other. The three analyses are about different topics, but the integrity orientation in which they function gives them a similar structure or rhetorical form.

## RATIONAL ARGUMENT AND ANALYSIS:
## INTIMACY'S *IN MEDIAS RES* AND HOLOGRAPHIC WHOLE

How different are the paradigms of rational argument and analysis arising from an intimacy orientation? Because intimacy analyzes relationships as internal rather than external, the parts of the whole cannot be separated from their relational overlap and the whole-as-parts paradigm is not adequate. Equally inadequate is the bipolarity paradigm because it defines things by isolating them from what they are *not*. And as we have seen earlier in this chapter, in a special sense intimacy understands that not-$x$ is intrinsically part of $x$'s nature. That is: within intimacy's orientation we cannot discuss the relations among the parts as something separate from the parts; the relation is in the overlap of the parts. What alternative can intimacy pose to the analytic and argumentative paradigms favored by integrity?

Within the intimacy orientation, one tends to analyze not in terms of poles but, rather, out of the *in medias res*. That is: analysis will not begin with the opposites and then locate phenomena in relation to these opposites; instead the phenomena themselves will be the beginning of the analysis. The opposite poles will be found within it and can be separated out as if in a centrifuge. It is important to note, however, that such a separation can never be complete or the very nature of the overlapping relation would be lost. That is: the polarities can never exist in themselves, even conceptually, as indivisible integers or units of integrity. The difference between integrity's bipolar paradigm and intimacy's paradigm of the *in medias res* might be sharpened by thinking of two different ways of characterizing the focal object "gray." For integrity, the analysis of gray will start with the opposites: white and black. Then it will proceed to analyze them as poles of a range, locating the particular shade of gray between them (in relation to how "close" the gray is to either white or black). For intimacy, by contrast, by studying gray we find within it the overlapping opposites of white and black. Variations in the overlap determine the shade. The difference is subtle but, as we will see later in this chapter, it has striking repercussions when it is carried over to metaphysics.

It might be helpful to return to our previous discussion of the God/humanity relation—but this time from within the orientation of intimacy instead of integrity. From intimacy's standpoint, it does not make sense to speak of God's nature or humanity's nature without analyzing the inseparability of the two. Without God, humanity would not be what it is; without humanity, God would not be what God is. The first part of this equation is probably clear enough in most faith traditions, but the latter may need an example. In an "emanation" theory of creation (as we find in Plotinus, for example), creation is not something God does (or did) as much as an aspect of God's own nature. In a Judeo-Christian context, an emphasis on God's creating humanity "in the image of God" may have the same rhetorical effect since it undermines the strict bifurcation between divine and human nature. In either case to talk about God involves to some extent talking about humanity and vice versa. This internal relation between God and humanity was not found in the integrity orientation's modes of analysis.

Integrity's whole-as-parts paradigm of analysis is also foreign to intimacy. Instead of integrity's Figure 27, intimacy would analyze reality into a series of overlapping relations as in Figure 30. Furthermore, intimacy's

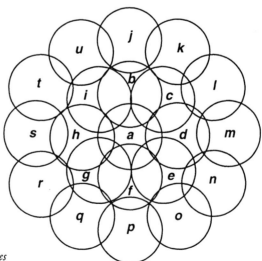

FIGURE 30. Intimacy's
Paradigm of *In Medias Res*

analysis is holographic or recursively fractal in its analysis—each part can only be understood as reflective of the whole. The part contains the whole as much as the whole contains the part. That is: the whole pattern *a–u* can be found within any of the individual circles *a, b, c,* and so forth. Alternatively, we can use an analogy from cellular biology. Insofar as each cell in my body shares the same DNA chain, each cell contains (and ultimately derives from) the genetic blueprint for the whole body. This fact is what makes cloning possible, for example. The whole and the part are in an intimate, internal relationship. One cannot be understood without the other. To clarify this difference between integrity and intimacy, let us consider some examples.

Consider the use of company logos on employee uniforms or team logos in sports. If we assembled all the people and buildings associated with, say, the McDonald's restaurant corporation, we would in one sense have the whole company. This would be integrity's analysis of the situation: the whole is defined as the individual parts and their external relations with each other. For intimacy, however, this analysis is inadequate. To the extent that McDonald's has established intimacy with its people and sites, the identification with McDonald's is part of what each person and each building is. In putting on the uniform with the golden arches, the person is expressing part of what she or he is. Dress, as we have seen, is part of style, an intimation of inner identity. A corporate goal is for customers to be part of the intimate group as well—to establish an affective relation to the restaurant chain. The customer is to feel at home when entering a McDonald's restaurant anywhere in the world. This is an aspect of the "belonging-with" characteristic of intimacy discussed in chapter 2. It is, therefore, not surprising to see a well-heeled American business executive duck into a Tokyo McDonald's for a late-night snack. To the weary traveler, McDonald's is part of home. For a child as well, eating at McDonald's restaurant means there is no struggle with menus one does not know or a place where behavior is unfamiliar. McDonald's is a place where children may feel they have expert knowledge.

A similar sense of personal identity may apply to the rabid sports fans whose emotions rise and fall with their team's success or failure. In Japan the identity between players and their fans is so intimate, in fact, that during a losing streak it is not uncommon for the team to come out before the game and formally apologize to the home fans for their lack of intensity and spirit. Cultural anthropologists have documented that when a Japanese is asked his occupation, the first response is typically "I work for the such-and-such corporation." Only further questioning will reveal whether one is a custodian, an engineer, or the CEO. In the United States, studies show, the answers are generally given in reverse order: the job one does is more central to one's individual identity than the company for which one works. The Japanese case suggests how strongly intimacy can define our identity in terms of the whole that we represent. The company logo on a Japanese business card or lapel pin is a holograph in which the whole is reflected in each of its parts—in this case in each employee. Indeed, the very idea of "representation" is shaded differently by intimacy and integrity. A congressperson in the U.S. House of Representatives is delegated authority through contract (the majority vote of the people in the congressional district). When a high school debate coach takes her team on the road, by contrast, there is often a mention of proper decorum, reminding the students they will be "representing" their school. That is: others will make judgments about the high school based on the team's behavior. The part intimately reflects the whole.

In intimacy, the relation is part of the relatents themselves. Part of the parent is the child, for example, and part of the child is the parent. Without my genetic parents, I cannot be. What I am intrinsically is, at least partly, a question about us (my parents and me). The relationship is internal, therefore, not external. It is not contractual—not a relationship that "I" have entered into either voluntarily or involuntarily. In tending to emphasize external relationship, however, integrity understands the "we" to be constituted by the "I's." It resembles the model depicted in Figure 12—that is, the "we" (the diagram as a whole) is a group of "I's" *(a–i)* bonded together in a special way, like the model of a molecule with the circular atoms held together by sticks in some configuration. By tending to emphasize internal relationship instead, intimacy understands the "we" as a partially coextensive set of "I's" like overlapping circles (Figure 13 or 14). If we analyze any "I" (*a* in the diagram), we find that part of the "I" overlaps with other "I's" *(b–i)*. That is: the "I" when fully analyzed is always embedded in a "we" shared by at least one other "I." One might say that "we" is part of what "I" am. We have already seen this in the discussion of knowledge as enmeshed in a praxis shared by the intimate community of expert knowers, the "we."

Incidentally, our discussion of intimacy's holographic paradigm suggests a limitation to our diagrams of internal relations—specifically the diagram of overlapping circles (Figure 9) and the diagram of broken intimacy (Figure 11). The overlap of *a* and *b,* insofar as the overlap is part of each, is not a discrete part. That is: $R$ is not a simple part of $a$ and $b$ in the whole-as-parts sense. Hence in thinking of "broken intimacy" as each relatent's losing part of itself, we occlude some of the complexity. We must add the idea that the $R$ is holographically reflected in the *whole* of $a$ and $b$. This implies that if $a$ and $b$ enter into an internal relation, then all of $a$ and all of $b$, not merely part of each, are involved. All of $a$ is reflected in its part, the internal overlap with $b$; and the overlap with $b$, as part of $a$, is reflected throughout $b$. By this reasoning, an internal relation is necessarily of the whole since the whole is in every part. When I share myself in the intimacy of love, I do not lose my identity into my lover, but the part I share reflects all of me. And all of me is reflected in this part. So that even if the intimacy is lost, I am still completely changed by my having been part of it.

## METAPHYSICS: INTEGRITY'S ATOMISM AND DUALISM

Metaphysics, technically speaking, is distinct from logic, analysis, or argument. There is no necessary connection between the way we think and the way reality is. Yet practically speaking, insofar as they are conceptual constructs, systems of metaphysics often mirror the basic structure of the rational analysis and arguments by which they develop. Let us continue this discussion by considering the implications for metaphysical systems that emphasize integrity's orientation as compared with those emphasizing intimacy.

Again, let us start with integrity and its paradigms of the whole-as-parts and bipolarity. Often the whole-as-parts paradigm for analysis carries over to the development of a metaphysics of atomism. That is: the way we structure analysis becomes a claim about how each reality is constructed. In such an atomistic metaphysics, primary units of being bond together externally and form the parts of a larger whole. In other words: in atomism the parts precede the whole not just logically but also ontologically. The atomist understands reality to be constructed from entities in external relation with each other. (Individuals create the political state; sentences or words form language; flora, fauna, weather, topography, geology, and so forth define nature; the rights and responsibilities of individuals give rise to ethics; sensations, physical processes, and neural connections constitute the body; and so forth.) To reiterate, then, the whole-as-parts is a paradigm of reasoning, arguing, and analyzing. But when it goes beyond that to become a claim about the nature of reality, it becomes a basis for a metaphysics of atomism.

If integrity's whole-as-parts paradigm of analysis and argument may be used to support metaphysical atomism, what kind of metaphysics might its bipolarity paradigm support? Clearly it would support a metaphysics of dualism. That is: once we assume that something can only be understood in relation to what-it-is-not, it is a small step to thinking that the actual (not merely conceptual) existence of something depends ontologically on its opposite. This is a move from duality (a mode of analysis of things in terms of opposites) to dualism (a kind of metaphysics which assumes that opposites exist as independent entities, each with its own ontological itegrity). Once someone accepts the epistemological or logical principle that we can only understand good insofar as it is distinguished from evil, for example, a metaphysics of the struggle between good and evil entities often emerges. This type of thinking has led to the ontological dualisms of being versus nonbeing, self versus other, humanity versus nature, mind versus body.

## METAPHYSICS: INTIMACY'S HOLISM AND
## THE YIN-YANG COALESCENCE OF OPPOSITES

A metaphysics developed within an intimacy orientation, by contrast, would have quite a different understanding of these relationships: opposites would overlap rather than be diametrically opposed to each other. Let us examine more closely how such a metaphysics might look. In simplest terms, if the intimacy's form of analysis—with its paradigm of the holographic—is projected into a metaphysics, this metaphysics takes on the character of holistic process and interdependence. Everything is related to everything else. Starting with the assumption that reality is a process in the midst of which we live, such a metaphysics would not dwell on issues of origins. If reality itself is an all-inclusive whole consisting of interdependent processes, it makes little sense to speculate about which entity sets the processes in motion. Any such creating entity would be outside the totalistic process and, by definition, not a reality itself. Such a metaphysics would probably not, therefore, have a philosophical narration of an event that brought independent, unrelated things (chaos) into external relation (order). Such a narrative would have to assume that things could exist without relation and would violate intimacy's understanding that things *(res)* exist only by being amidst *(in medias)* other things. We find here a metaphysical holism. As a metaphysical system, monism claims that reality is an undifferentiated One; dualism claims that it is Two; pluralism claims that it is Many. In contrast, holism (sometimes called "totalism") maintains that reality is a differentiated One. The parts really exist, but never as individuals separate from the whole. To some this may seem paradoxical. But if we recall intimacy's cluster of overlapping circles (Figure 30), it is perfectly intelligible. No circle can exist as what it is without the interdependence with other circles. And this, in turn, entails further circles ad infinitum.

Intimacy's forms of metaphysics can also be said to be basically "ecological." If we think of the difference in the etymologies of the terms "environmental" and "ecological," we can better focus on the difference between integrity and intimacy. Insofar as its etymology suggests "surrounding," the word "environment" implies a metaphysical framework like Figure 27. The environment *(b–y)* is what is around me *(a)*, that is, the circum-stances—the "what stands around me"—within which I live. At best I can be a discrete part of the whole. "Ecology's" etymology, by contrast, is the "study of home" (*"eco"* from the Greek for "home," *oikos*). Hence the ecological model suggests where I belong: in the interdependent system of all things. Figure 30 is better than Figure 27 for picturing this. The ecology is the interdependent network *(a–u)* from which I *(a)* cannot be separated. Such a metaphysical model is more likely to arise out of an intimacy than an integrity orientation.

Insofar as intimacy's forms of holistic and *in-medias-res* metaphysics reject the bipolar analysis suggesting metaphysical dualism, it is reminiscent of the Chinese model of yin and yang. The yin-yang relation is often depicted as Figure 31. The yang (the white) never exists purely as yang—there is always some yin (the black) in it—and vice versa. No thing exists alone in and of itself without significant overlap with other things—

FIGURE 31. Yin-Yang

including things that seem to be in opposition to it. "Substance"—in the usual sense of being an independent, integral entity—simply has no place in this model. Furthermore, as the relationships in intimate relations undergo change (the yin-yang model is one of flux not stasis), they affect all the other relationships with which they overlap (the holographic paradigm again). Overall this leads to a metaphysical system in which each thing interrelates with at least something else and perhaps ultimately everything else. As a consequence, studying the smallest thing (a grain of sand) yields holographically or recursively an insight into the greatest whole (the universe). Following this reasoning, we may understand the whole as a set of interdependent internal relations (the political state as the will of the people, nature as ecosystem, experience as the mutual expression of self and world, and so forth). We will explore the normative consequences of such a view in the next chapter.

## THE BIG PICTURE

We have dealt in some detail with the differences in epistemology, rational argument, and metaphysics that would result from foregrounding either integrity or intimacy. In concluding this chapter, let us stand back from the details of this analysis to see the larger picture. In particular let us pause to think about the *practical* difference it would make if we were to favor one orientation over the other. This will serve both as a summary of what we have said and as a broad depiction of the differences.

One way to characterize the differences is to ask what kind of knowledge counts most in each paradigm. For integrity, we have knowledge as *epistēmē;* for intimacy we have something closer to *phrónēsis.* That is: it is a difference between what our modern Western epistemological systems call "knowledge" and what is often called "practical wisdom" (or any of an array of related models such as "tacit knowledge" or "expert knowledge"). Integrity tends to think of the world as something external to be managed through knowledge. Intimacy, however, tends to see the self and world as interlinking—the goal being to develop a sense of belonging *with* the world, feeling at home in it. The integrity model understands knowledge as being able to capture something "out there" through concepts, principles, and words. Knowledge connects one *to* the world; it is the external relation between the polarities of knower and known. The intimacy model of knowledge, by contrast, understands knowledge to re-side in the interface *between* self and world. It is embodied in persons embedded within their intimate community of praxis and knowledge. Studying the world entails studying oneself as well; it begins not with a polarity but an *in medias res.* Such knowledge is communicated not through the discovery and learning of principles, but by apprenticing oneself to an expert or a master in order to discover by imitating, to learn by doing. In the intimacy model, the self is a holographic image of the whole and knowledge occurs where world and self intersect.

As noted previously, my goal in this book is not primarily to gain an understanding of any particular culture or subculture. I hope, rather, to give an analysis that may be useful in describing or comparing various cultures and subcultures. To illuminate some of the issues of this chapter, we can resort to an example from the interface of Japanese and Western culture. It seems to embody the difference in epistemological goals between a culture or subculture that emphasizes intimacy and one that emphasizes integrity. Some years ago I spent a year as a visiting professor at Harvard University. I happened to have the opportunity to meet several students from the Business School, including a few Japanese. I remember asking the Japanese why they had come to the United States to get an M.B.A. Surely, by that time, there was no theory or information being taught at Harvard that was not already available in Japan. Their answer surprised me. They informed me that they were not there to learn any particular theory, but rather to form personal relationships with those who would be leaders in American business thirty years from now. Expecting to serve a similar role in their own country, they believed it would be important to know some of these Americans personally and to have shared experiences with them over a period of many years before they had to negotiate and cooperate as leaders of their own respective spheres. This long-term relationship would cultivate a deeper level of mutual understanding when it really counted.

Obviously I had been thinking in terms of a model in which the student was to learn the principles of how the business world operates. But the Japanese graduate students were thinking in terms of forging relationships that would create an internal connection between them and their future foreign counterparts. Because learning how to manage was learned in Japan under the tutelage of a mentor, to understand American managers one had to be with them personally in order to get to know them and how they were trained. At about this time Japan's economic success was striking and American businesspeople wanted to learn the "secrets of

Japanese management." Books galore appeared, exploring the "princi-ples" Japanese managers were supposedly following. Yet very few Ameri-cans went to Japan to be actually trained as Japanese managers. In short: Americans were looking for the *principles* applied by the knowledgeable manager; the Japanese were looking for the *people* who embody and ex-press the knowledge. The Americans wanted to have someone shed light on Japanese management principles; the Japanese wanted to acquire the dark, expert knowledge arising from common praxis.

Besides illuminating the difference in how education and knowledge were understood, this example from the training of Japanese and Amer-ican managers also suggests a difference in the way people interrelate and how they treat each other. It is in fact a difference in how ethics might be understood. In the next chapter we move from what-is to what-ought-to-be—from the world of knowledge to the world of value as represented by aesthetics, ethics, and politics.

# CHAPTER 5

# THE NORMATIVE DIMENSIONS OF INTIMACY AND INTEGRITY

## AESTHETICS, ETHICS, AND POLITICS

Starting with the basic orientations of intimacy and integrity, in the preceding chapter we developed two alternative directions for the course of philosophy in the fields of epistemology, argument or analysis, and metaphysics. In effect we explored how differently we might understand what-is depending on which orientation we foregrounded as most fundamental, important, and worthy of analysis. In this chapter we will continue this project by considering the normative domain of what-ought-to-be. In other words: we will take what we have learned about how intimacy and integrity might understand the descriptive givenness of the world and proceed to see how their axiologies might prescriptively shape that world through human action. Specifically we will consider how foregrounding either intimacy or integrity may affect the development of aesthetics, ethics, and politics.

In itself the analysis of what-ought-to-be can be quite abstract, but as soon as it becomes the basis for practical values realized in action, our sense of what-ought-to-be has to be applied to our knowledge of what-is. To know what to do, to determine what is possible, to see how things can be done—all involve a binocular vision on what-is and what-ought-to-be. If it is to be persuasive and effective, a justification for an action or a call to action will generally proceed from the audience's dominant orientation. In an intimacy-dominant culture, for example, the normative power of the political rhetoric may have most efficacy when its analysis of the problem—its interpretation of the what-is—is formulated within the familiar structures of the dominant epistemologies, forms of argument, and metaphysics. In other words: the normative may be at odds with the descriptive—what-ought-to-be may not coincide with what-is—but the normative and descriptive still cohere best and lead to an agreed upon course of action when they share the same orientation. This helps to explain why intimacy-dominant cultures and integrity-dominant cultures often find cooperation so difficult: they find each other's reasoning inscrutable or "beside the point." In failed attempts at coordinated action, the misunderstandings across orientations lead to claims that the other side is being duplicitous. Sharing a basis within discourse is a basis for trust.

Before proceeding to our analysis of the fields of aesthetics, ethics, and politics, therefore, it might be useful to have the major points of the last chapter available to us in a list. Table 2 should be helpful. Keeping in mind these characteristics, let us now turn to the normative philosophical disciplines of aesthetics, ethics, and politics.

## AESTHETICS

In moving from the descriptive to the prescriptive, let us start with aesthetics, the creative alteration of things to express a valued relation that is not obvious (or not present at all) in their brute givenness. Our goal here is not to develop a theory of aesthetics per se but to see how the orientations develop an approach and terminology for analyzing, understanding, or developing aesthetics.

### Integrity's Version

Given its authorized descriptive paradigms, it is no surprise that integrity's artistic relation is understood through duality or bipolarity. First there is the polarity of artist and world as mediated by the external relation: the artistic expression. The work of art is the artist's response to the world, taking the world as presented and remolding it into an innovative, creative expression. The artist envisions something that is not but should be. That act itself has two parts: the epistemic judgment that something does not exist and the normative judgment that it should. Then the artist

Table 2. Comparison of the Descriptive Domains of Integrity and Intimacy

| Integrity | Intimacy |
|---|---|
| **EPISTEMOLOGY** | |
| 1. Publicly verifiable objectivity. | 1. Nonpublic objectivity; knowledge limited to intimate circle of experts. |
| 2. Knowledge does not necessarily affect knower or known. | 2. Knowing affects knower and known. |
| 3. Correspondence theory of truth. | 3. Assimilation theory of truth. |
| 4. Language as referential (may lead to theory of propositions). | 4. Expression arises out of mutual effect of knower and known. |
| **RATIONAL ARGUMENT OR ANALYSIS** | |
| 1. Whole-as-parts paradigm. | 1. Holographic paradigm: whole in every part. |
| 2. Analysis through bipolarity paradigm (opposites as polar opposites defining what is between them). | 2. Analysis out of *in media res* (opposites abstracted out of single undifferentiated whole). |
| 3. Discrete "individual" ("building block" necessary to logical analysis); emphasis on independence. | 3. No discrete "individual" necessary ("ecological" or "systems" model); emphasis on interdependence. |
| **METAPHYSICS** | |
| 1. Whole-as-parts paradigm ontologized as atomism. | 1. Holograph paradigm ontologized as web of interdependent processes. |
| 2. Bipolarity paradigm ontologized as dualism. | 2. Opposites interpenetrate as in yin-yang model (Figure 31). |

creatively makes that something real. By this process, the artist's production is added to the world of fact and value.

Concurrently there is a bipolar social relation: the artist and audience are discrete entities connected through the artistic expression. The artist is the major causal agent—in effect using the work of art as a bridge between one's own creative intention and the audience. In the integrity orientation, therefore, one tends to think of the artist as having a subjectivity (a creative intentionality) that transforms the objectivity of the world into something expressive of a new relation or meaning. Using his or her creativity, the artist works the what-is into something new. For example:

the landscape designer's creativity turns ordinary plants and rocks into a garden; the poet's creativity transforms ordinary words into combinations that evoke new meanings, enhancing the audience's insight into the world and its possibilities; the painter's creativity transforms a natural object, color, or shape into a new configuration that leads the observer to see a relation not otherwise manifest.

In all these ways the integrity of both the artist and the world are maintained. The artist retains autonomy and individuality through her or his creative expression. The artist is not confined to what-is and can reconstitute things according to her or his own creative impulse. By calling this addition "subjective," the integrity orientation often uses its bipolar form of analysis to develop a dualistic ontology bifurcating the world into the realm of fact and the realm of aesthetic expression. The work of art is something not only additional to, but also essentially different from, the so-called objective reality. In many aesthetic theories of this sort, even the work of art itself, once completed, has its own integrity independent of the artist. It stands alone in its newly attained objectivity ("the art object") as a thing in the world to be studied and interpreted "subjectively" by an audience. Even the artist's original intent, the volitional vector that first directed the work of art into the world of audience, may be irrelevant to the audience's critical interpretation. In short: the work of art becomes an end in itself and stands for itself in its own integrity, independent of both artist and audience. Figure 32 is a way of depicting some of these relations within the integrity orientation. Again we should remember that the ensuing discussion will not be an aesthetic theory itself but, rather, the orientation that serves as a starting point for theory. Aestheticians may disagree over the precise relation between intent and interpretation, for example, or between world and art. Yet so long as the theories consider these relations to be more external than internal, they still operate—however different they may be in detail—from an integrity orientation. The orientation does not give us a theory of what art is or a judgment about which art is good so much as it yields the basic conceptual framework for talking about these issues.

## Intimacy's Version

Now let us turn to the kind of aesthetic that might emerge from foregrounding intimacy instead of integrity. For intimacy, the artist would be conceived as not existing separately from the world but intersecting with

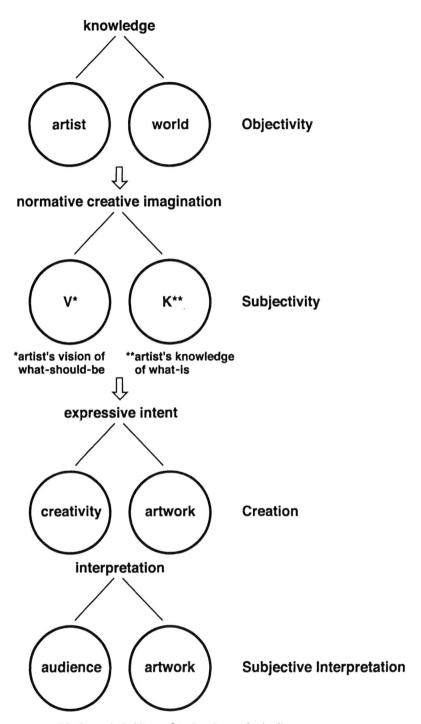

FIGURE 32. Integrity's View of Artist, Artwork, Audience

it. The creativity would emerge not from the artist but from the interface of artist and world. If the artist were to make a painting of the sparrow on the tree branch, the sparrow and tree together with the artist—their overlap in an internal relation—would be the source of the creativity. This suggests that, at least in some sense, art is not just the expression of the artist but also part of the world's self-expression. After all, if the artist is part of the world, part of nature, then the artist's expression is, at least in this respect, part of nature's own expression. The world is using one of its parts, the artist, as the medium for its artistic self-articulation.

Because the relation between artist and world is internal, there is no sense of integrity's bifurcation between fact and value or between objectivity and subjectivity. In fact, intimacy's way of knowing and its way of artistic creativity are fundamentally very similar in that they arise out of the overlap and interdependency of the world and the person. (See Figure 33.) As we have seen, integrity tends to identify creativity with individual freedom: the artist is untouched and therefore autonomous and free. In this freedom of expression, art achieves its subjective creativity, allowing the artist to rework the givenness of the world. Creativity is a way for the artist to contact the world and an audience. The intimacy orientation, by contrast, tends to identify creativity with a naturalness or with a responsive spontaneity that works *with* the world in creating the work of art. If the human being is a creative expression of nature, then the human being's creativity also derives from nature in some way. Creativity allows the artist to overlap with the world and the audience. When creativity is viewed as this overlap, we can say that without the artist's creativity, the world is incomplete—and without the world's creativity, the artist is incomplete. The relation between what-is (fact) and what-should-be (value) is not construed in a bipolar, dualistic manner. Instead it is more of the interdependent, yin-yang type of metaphysics depicted in

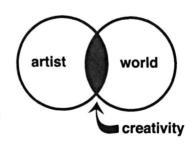

FIGURE 33. Intimacy's
View of Creativity

Figure 31. That is: in the middle of the artist's passive sensitivity (yin) is the expressive kernel of active expression (yang), and in the world's expressiveness (yang) is its opening to be receptive (yin) to the artist's creative contribution. Viewed in this light, the yin-yang diagram exposes the mutual interdependence and interpenetration of artistic expression and the world.

Intimacy's aesthetic recalls the story about Michelangelo and the creation of the statue *David* recounted in chapter 1. Michelangelo "saw" the image of David in the marble block; there was resonance between Michelangelo's creative sensitivity and the nature of the marble. Michelangelo responded to the block's inherent grain and shape as an expression of what could be. Out of this response—this overlap between Michelangelo and the physical object—emerged the statue *David*, what should be. To achieve such responsiveness, the artist needs to learn how to read what nature is trying to express—a skill that is not readily achieved through intellectual study but is typically part of a praxis that frees one first of all from the boundaries of one's own ego. Such a praxis is often incorporated, taken holistically into the psycho-somatic-spiritual self, under the tutelage of a master. The apprentice learns to sense what the master senses by watching the master respond in a special way to the given—the given of the world generally and the given of the artistic medium specifically used in the work of art. It is an objective but nonpublic way of intersecting with, and responding with, the world. Pursuing this line of thought further, an intimacy orientation might even suggest that art is a way of knowing the world, including oneself as part of the world. In the intimacy orientation, epistemology and aesthetics come together. The artist achieves a form of expert knowledge. Intimacy's aesthetics and epistemology involve being responsive to the world, being self-consciously part of the world, working with the world in order to achieve the expression of the world. Through the meditative artistic praxis, the artist softens the hard shell of the ego and opens oneself to the world until one's identity is enhanced by the overlap with the world. The artist, by being in touch with the world, is also touched by it. Reality expresses itself through the artist. This notion is reminiscent of chapter 1's example of the pianist: at one point it seems the pianist is no longer playing the music but, rather, the music is playing through the pianist.

Our consideration of aesthetics in the intimacy orientation sheds further light on the issue of subjectivity and objectivity raised previously.

When we spoke of "objectivity" in intimacy's forms of knowing, we understood this term in the context of entailing agreement from other appropriate judges. For integrity, the set of appropriate judges was very large—in theory, any rational person with even the most basic background in the relevant field. For integrity, objectivity entails that if two rational people knew the methods or rules for judging, they would come to the same conclusion. Hence integrity's model of knowledge is public and objective. "Subjectivity," from integrity's standpoint, means the judgment is strictly one's own without the expectation of common agreement. Let us compare the senses of objectivity and subjectivity from an intimacy orientation.

As discussed in the preceding chapter, intimacy too claims objectivity for its judgments. As in the case of integrity, the expectation in making a claim for objectivity is agreement from other qualified judges. Unlike integrity, however, intimacy defines the set of qualified judges more restrictively, limiting it to "expert" judges. This observation led us to consider intimacy's form of knowledge as being "objective but nonpublic." What, then, about subjectivity within the intimacy orientation? It has the same definition it has in the integrity orientation: a subjective judgment is strictly one's own without the expectation of common agreement. For an intimacy orientation, this kind of judgment comes from outside the intimate group of fellow experts—those who have assimilated intimate knowledge through common praxis. To intimacy, therefore, subjectivity is typically an egoistic expression arising in isolation from the artistic community and the developed modes of sensitivity.

These contrasts underscore a difference between intimacy's and integrity's take on the relations between knowing and artistic creation. For intimacy, the two are close in nature. But for integrity, there is an important gap between them. For intimacy, art has an objectively knowable basis; for integrity, it usually does not. Integrity separates the normative world of value (which includes artworks) and the world of being (in which artworks can exist materially but not artistically). Because of this difference, integrity's challenge is to explain how there can be any objectivity in art at all (in judging that Shakespeare's *Hamlet,* for example, is a better play than his *Troilus and Cressida*). Intimacy's challenge is to explain how true innovation in art is even possible (in recognizing the development of a "new school" in art history, for example, that seems to break with tradition of the artistic community possessing expert knowledge). This suggests why different philosophical traditions often spend much of their time exploring different questions rather than finding different answers to the same questions.

A related contrast between the intimacy and integrity orientations takes us back to the observation that integrity regards the work of art as having its own integrity—its own expressive meaning independent of what the artist may have intended. Viewed in this light, the work of art has its own presence and the members of the audience may engage this presence with their own subjective creative impulses. For integrity, the audience's interpretation of the work of art is fundamentally parallel to the artist's subjectively creative response to the world. That is: the artist has made the work of art part of what-is, no longer just what-ought-to-be, part of something actual instead of merely possible. This creates an art world in the special sense that the aesthetic audience can respond creatively to the existence of the work of art and construe from it what ought-to-be according to the audience's own normative subjectivity. For intimacy, by contrast, the work of art would be viewed as ineluctably part of the artist and the expressive situation that "naturally" or "spontaneously" gave rise to it. In an artistic piece of pottery, the potter is as much the medium as is the clay. The intimacy audience values the great work of art not so much for itself but as an intrinsic part of the artistic expression with which it is in an internal, even holographic, relation. What the artist has become is inseparable from the coming into being of the work of art. The artist himself or herself is a work of art. In knowing the work of art, one necessarily knows the artist. In this context, it is not surprising that in the *Platform Sutra* a Zen master may know a student's state of mind by reading the student's poem. Nor is it surprising that in some forms of religious art (an Orthodox Christian icon, for example, or a Native American or Tibetan sand mandala) the artist must be a person of spiritual accomplishment to be allowed to produce the artistic expression for the religious community.

Let us consider further the audience of the work of art. In integrity's forms of aesthetics, the viewers, listeners, or readers have their own inviolable standpoint quite apart from the artistic act of creation and the final product. Thus the audience has the privilege of building whatever relation—whatever subjective interpretation—that seems warranted and personally satisfying. In such a context the audience expects the art critics to disagree and they in turn have the privilege of taking away from this disagreement whatever they wish. In effect, the art critic is involved in a creative, subjective act—free to find a new meaning to connect audience and the work of art. The art criticism then becomes a product itself, a thing in the world, to which the members of the audience can form their own subjective responses. In intimacy's aesthetic, however, the spectator, audience, or critic stands, as one would expect, in an *internal* relation with the work of art: the audience overlaps with the work of art. As the artist has to be in touch with the world in order to be touched by it, the audience of the work of art must also be in touch with art to be touched by it. And in being touched by it, one senses the artist's touch as well. The work of art is an expressive *intimation* of the natural self-expression of the artist-world.

By "intimation" I mean that something is being made known, but it is being made known in such a way that only intimates will get it. In some respects an intimation is like an insider joke. Imagine a group of friends and someone makes an inside joke. The insiders all laugh, but a guest in the group, someone outside this intimate circle, doesn't get it and just gives a quizzical look. Realizing the outsider doesn't know the context—the previous events that give the present comment its humor—one insider may try to explain this context in a discursive way. The outsider comes to understand the context, but still does not find the joke to be funny. He understands the joke, but he does not get it. An insider might then say, "Well, you had to be there." But where is "there"? Not physically there, obviously, but there within the intimate social circle. Suppose another person belonging to this circle happens by. An insider tells her the joke. She laughs. She was not there physically when the joke was told, but she is an insider to the group. So she not only understands, but she also gets the joke.

We need to pause a moment to think about this phenomenon of "getting it." Why is the joke funny to an insider but not to an outsider even when the joke is completely explained? Once the outsider gets the explanation, certainly, there is nothing significant about the joke that is left unknown. So it is not a matter of ignorance. The important difference is the way the joke conjures up the memory, knowledge, and context for people in the intimate circle. The joke invokes or evokes the background knowledge of the insiders in a sudden and unexpected way. Consequently, the insiders laugh. For the outsider, though, the background knowledge and context are explained rather than invoked. The explanation lacks the power to make the background suddenly appear and instead delineates it gradually and in parts through a discursive account. Unlike the

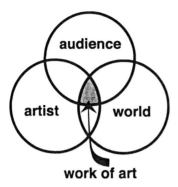

**audience**

**artist**    **world**

**work of art**

FIGURE 34. Intimacy's View
of Artist, Artwork, Audience

joke itself, the explanation is not holistic. The explanation is public and it places the outsider in the position of knowing the context from the outside. The joke's humor itself, however, is nonpublic; it draws on what is already shared by the insiders. And it brings something out of this shared nonpublic internal relation in an abrupt and striking way. So the insiders laugh. To them the joke is objectively funny, though not in a publicly accessible manner.

Analogously the audience of a work of art, when understood from the standpoint of an aesthetics of intimacy, is invited to "get with it"—to enter the intimate circle so one can "get" the intimation that is the artwork. The audience joins in with the responsiveness of the artist, the world, and the work of art much as the insider joins in the laughter of the intimate circle when the joke is told. In a sense, the art of an aesthetic of intimacy is always a performance art—a performance in which the audience not only watches but participates. In this respect, we could diagram this aesthetic as Figure 34, where the shaded area—the work of art—is the overlap of artist, world, and audience. If you "get" the work of art, you have intimate access to all three circles.

An example from the East Asian painting tradition may be helpful in exemplifying the aesthetics of intimacy. Many Westerners are quite familiar with the Sung-dynasty style of ink-wash landscape paintings. These are the well-known pictures depicting a landscape of huge mountains, often a river, and a tiny person somewhere in the vast expanse, perhaps on a boat in the water or in a hermitage on the side of the mountain. Our interest here, however, is the Chinese text that is often written in a blank space near the top of the painting. This writing is typically a poem. But sometimes the poem is written by someone other than the painter of the landscape. Perhaps even a century might pass between the painting of the landscape and the insertion of the text. It might seem to us that this behavior is bizarre. The integrity of the painting seems to have been violated. It might strike us as analogous to letting patrons of the Metropolitan Museum of Art add some personal graffiti to a painting by Monet or Rembrandt. But of course, in the Chinese case not just anyone is allowed to write on the painting. Only a person with a highly refined aesthetic sensitivity to both painting and poetry, not to mention an accomplished style of calligraphy, would be able to do so. That is: only an individual with a mastery of an artistic praxis might so intimately join in with the working of the artwork. The key point for us to notice is the performative aspect of this practice. The spectator is not only invited into the work of art but may also contribute something of one's own to it. The "paint-ing" is an event, not a finished thing. (Perhaps a more suitable term for the latter would be a "paint-ed.") The performance of this artistic event is in the internal relation between artist and audience. Indeed in the case of the landscape painting, the spectator participates not only in the landscape painting but also in the calligraphic text. The work of art opens itself to an ever widening circle of intimacy—a circle of people who get it. The audience of a work of art is part of the work of art and, indeed, is in an intimate relation with the artist as well. As the natural self-expression of what-is, as the product of years of disciplined praxis, as the fruit of studying (and studying with) the masters, artistry is intrinsically a social act.

## ETHICS

Let us turn now to ethics, the philosophical field that asks fundamental questions about how a person should treat the other (whether the other be human or nonhuman). Again, because the integrity and intimacy orientations have radically different ways of characterizing self and other, this affects the way in which moral values can be articulated, analyzed, and evaluated.

### *Integrity's Version*

Again let us begin with integrity. If one understands the relation between self and other to be an external relation, then ethics addresses this external relation, examining how it should be. From integrity's standpoint, the most important norm, not surprisingly, is that relations should recognize and preserve the integrity of all individuals involved. This overriding moral mandate applies whether the other is human or nonhuman. First let us consider the case of how we should treat other people.

To preserve integrity, I should treat other people as autonomous agents having the privilege of being able to determine their own actions freely, including choosing the relationships into which they enter. This suggests further, as Kant pointed out, that I should never reduce the other person merely to a means for my own ends. As the English idiom goes, in a relation of integrity one should not "use" other people. The other is entitled to have his or her own ends and to work toward them with autonomy. How can one test whether a proposed relation is going to maintain the integrity of both parties? The test is simple: if the proposed action would really preserve the integrity of both parties, each party would be theoretically willing to reverse the proposed action. That is: to test whether the action I propose would violate the other's integrity, I need only imagine that the other were to act that way toward me. This is the normative basis of a number of ethical theories—from Jesus' (or Confucius') golden rule, to Immanuel Kant's categorical imperative, to John Rawls' theory of justice. All have in one way or another affirmed that for a relation $aRb$ to be ethical, one should be willing to enter this relationship without foreknowledge as to whether one will be the $a$ or the $b$.

Such an ethics of integrity lends itself well to the development of formal principles. Because the ideal ethical relation is external to the parties involved, the specifics of the two parties have their own integrity outside the relationship. So it makes no difference theoretically who the $a$ and $b$ are when they enter into such an external ethical relationship. This allows the nature of the relationship to be universalized such that it can be expressed in formal moral principles or rules. That is: if an external relation is ethical, it is equally so whether the situation involves $aRb$, or $bRa$, or $cRd$, and so on. In the integrity orientation, what makes the relationship ethical is the $R$—not the $a$, $b$, $c$, or $d$. When this $R$ is abstracted out of the concrete context, it can be formulated as a universal ethical maxim or principle. Again, we can view Kant's theory of the categorical imperative as based on precisely this insight. To test the validity of a proposed moral maxim, according to Kant, we must be able to imagine it is not simply a hypothetical but a categorical. That is: we must be able to imagine consistently that it could be a universal law binding on all human interaction.

*Intimacy's Version*_____

What about the ethics of intimacy? How would ethical behavior toward others be articulated, analyzed, and evaluated in this orientation? In intimacy, of course, one starts not with discrete entities of self and other connected by an external relation but with the overlap of self and other. When I act on the other I am—at least to some extent—acting on myself. As integrity's ethics seek to preserve or even enhance the integrity of the people involved, intimacy seeks to preserve or enhance the intimacy between the people involved.

In the intimacy orientation, ethics demands that I open myself to the other and accept the opening of the other to me. The basis of such a morality is in making the plight of the other, at least in part, *my* plight. Conversely my well-being, my happiness, my joy, is only mine insofar as it is at least partially shared with another. I avoid harming others because such actions harm me in some way as well. In early Indian Buddhism, the morally functional terms *"kusala"* and *"akusala"* mean, not "good" and "evil," but "skillful" and "unskillful." Early Buddhism assumed that to engage the other morally is to take care of oneself, as well, especially one's own progress toward enlightenment. To take another example: Jesus said, "Love thy neighbor as thyself" (Mark 12:31). Intimacy's gloss on this statement would be that to love one's neighbor, when properly understood and enacted, is also ultimately a form of self-love. For intimacy, love of neighbor and love of self are internally related. The Mahāyāna Buddhist, along similar lines, emphasizes that we need to get beyond sympathy to reach compassion. Ultimately, sympathy is an external relation in that I feel sadness and regret in the face of suffering that is not mine. In compassion, however, I feel *with* the other person; the suffering of the other is also part of me. In the Buddhist text the *Vimalakīrti Sūtra,* when the sage Vimalakīrti was ill a bodhisattva was sent down from the heavens to ask why he was sick. He replied, "I am sick because beings are sick." Compassion breaks the shell of the ego so that the pain of others enters our own being.

As we have seen, integrity's emphasis on external relation naturally leads to an ethics of principles. What follows, then, from intimacy's emphasis on internal relation? Rather than abstracting general principles that would apply to any person in the same circumstances, intimacy involves us in the particularities of the overlap with the other. When acting morally according to this model, I enter—at least in part—into the situation of the other. Thus the ethics is "situational" as well as guided by love. As we recall, within intimacy's orientation knowledge is affectively charged. So there is a natural transition from intimately knowing another person's plight to empathizing with it in a responsive manner. There need be no recourse to evaluating abstract or general moral principles. Intimacy's ethics and epistemology are, therefore, inescapably linked. As we saw in chapter 4, intimacy's version of knowledge is not a relation connecting self and world but an overlap between self and world. Therefore, for intimacy, if I know another's suffering, it becomes part of me. This is expressed explicitly in Mahāyāna Buddhism's claim that wisdom and compassion are intimately related.

We find such an intimacy orientation in the didactic stories of many religious traditions, including both Christianity and Buddhism. The New Testament, for instance, informs us that Jesus frequently violated the literal law of his Jewish community out of acts of compassion—to help the afflicted woman on the Sabbath (Luke 13:15), for example, or to disperse the crowd about to stone the adulteress (John 8:1–11). The technique in the latter case is particularly revealing. Jesus stopped the stoning by simply saying: "Let he who is without sin cast the first stone." In so doing Jesus made the potential executioners see the overlap between themselves and the woman so that their principled moral outrage at the external other was transformed into a compassion arising out of the woman's—and their own—shared situation.

There is a Buddhist story with a similar moral and similar morality. Two monks, wandering the forest in the most austere period of their self-discipline, came to a ford in the river where they met a beautiful young woman. The woman said that the current was too strong for her and asked for help in getting across. The first monk started to say no—that they were forbidden to have any physical contact with women at this point in their training. Before he could get this all out, however, the second monk hoisted the woman up on his shoulders and carried her across. They bade the woman good-bye and went on their respective ways. After some time, the first monk said, "I can't believe what you did. I'll have to report you to the abbot for breaking the rules." The second monk replied, "How tired you must be! When I got the woman across the river, I put her down. But you, you've been carrying her all this way!" The first monk was trapped by integrity's submission to the rules whereas the second monk responded to the immediate situation out of intimacy's compassion.

We should not make the error of thinking that intimacy's ethics of responsiveness necessarily requires an *immediate* response, however. Intimacy's response can be deliberative, but its analysis will follow the orientation of intimacy rather than integrity. We may find an example of this
within certain forms of Western medieval casuistry, for example. Such
casuistry analyzed moral predicaments through the practical wisdom
achieved from praxis in the art of moral adjudication. Used in cases where
there was no clear mandate derived from an explicit moral/divine principle or commandment, casuistry started with the *in medias res* and looked
for moral guidance internal to the facts of the case. Since the imprint of
God was understood to be in everything, the goal was to "discover"
God's will in the details of the specific. In effect, value was found intimately within the facts. In cases where this value could be generalized, it
might sometimes be raised to the abstract level of "natural law" and then
be used to guide future decisions (making the case a precedent for subsequent deliberation). Over the centuries, this policy led to the development of a comprehensive system of laws to be morally obeyed without
further discovery—basically an integrity system. Yet by casuistry's methods, even if the law could not be extracted unambiguously in this way the
moral case could still be decided "on its own merits." (Note the normative language: the evaluation of merit arises out of the facts and is not
external to it.) In this respect, casuistry often operated from an intimacy
orientation.

To put all this in another way, we could say: in the integrity orientation ethics is primarily a morality of principles; in the intimacy orientation, however, ethics is a morality of love. Integrity's moral demand is to
be *fair* to the other person; intimacy's is to *be there for* the other person.
Integrity generates a morality of responsibility, whereas intimacy generates a morality of responsiveness. Now let us see how these ethical orientations apply to relations between human beings and nonhuman things.
To make this concrete, let us develop our explanation around an example
explored briefly in the last chapter—namely, the relation between humanity and nature. Since our concern now is ethics, we will focus on how an
ethics of integrity and an ethics of intimacy might approach the issue of
environmental or ecological ethics.

For integrity's ethics, nature is that toward which we human beings
have a responsibility. Our relationship to nature is external and bipolar insofar as our species is different from the rest of nature; we stand in a distinctive place vis-à-vis the natural world. How? First of all, as a species we

are a special breed of engineers. We alter nature. But unlike other engineering species, our actions are capable of complex self-reflection. We act not only out of simple instinct but also conscious intentions allowing us to foresee the results of our actions. Hence we are capable of responsibility. As the only species capable of consciously changing the entire ecosystem of the planet, as the only species capable of consciously destroying virtually all life on earth, we play a special role vis-à-vis the natural order. We have special responsibilities. We can understand the patterns of destruction we have initiated and can fathom their negative impact on the natural order of things. Many believe we humans have collectively violated the integrity of nature; we have raped the earth. Yet the environmental ethicist of an integrity orientation argues that it is a human responsibility to be good stewards of the earth—to use our special capacities to heal the disrupted natural order. In summation: the integrity orientation of environmental ethics sees humans as distinctive and special. Because of this special external relationship to nature, human beings can locate in themselves the blame for environmental destruction and accept the responsibility for fixing it. Such an integrity-based environmental ethics calls for humans to restore the integrity of nature that they have violated.

The analysis is quite different when we start from intimacy. From this orientation, humans and the natural order overlap. As noted in our discussion of intimacy's metaphysical orientation in chapter 4, the perspective is ecological rather than environmental. We humans are part of nature, not separate from it. It follows, then, that humanity's ecologically destructive actions are, at least in part, nature's self-destruction. This parallels intimacy's aesthetic claim that the artist's creativity is, in part, nature's creativity. Our place in nature is, in this special sense, no different from that of other species who destroy in order to live—the soldier ants and the locusts, for example. Because "responsibility" is integrity's concept, it is unpersuasive to argue within intimacy's orientation that the preservation of nature is humanity's *responsibility*. To an environmentalist weaned on integrity ethics, this "lack of responsibility" may seem outrageous. Yet as we have seen in our discussion of intimacy's ethics toward people, this "lack of responsibility" is to be seen in light of an emphasis on *responsiveness*. To understand how intimacy could generate an ecological ethics, let us consider two anecdotes.

The first episode occurred when I was hiking in the woods of northern Wisconsin several years ago. I came to a rise in the terrain and saw only the tops of a large group of trees on the other side of the hill I was climbing. Although it was midsummer, all the trees were obviously dead. The branches were a leafless, barren, bleached white. I wondered what natural catastrophe we human beings had wrought. When I got to the top of the rise, I saw that the group of dead trees extended for about three acres: a sign of complete, though localized, devastation. What had caused the death of the trees? A closer look revealed that a family of beavers had settled there, building a dam and lodge in the large brook running through the area. This dam had created an artificial pond, submerging the root systems of the vegetative life. The trees had died from the rotting of their roots. The question is: were the beavers ethically *responsible* for the devastation? The term seems inappropriate. The beavers, while certainly the cause of the event, were not in any way moral agents. They had not—indeed could not have—deliberated over the situation, finally deciding that their comfort was more important than the life of a few acres of trees. They were just beavers, doing what beavers do. Nothing could be more natural. These actions were part of the natural way of things, not a violation of nature.

The second anecdote takes us to a busy traffic intersection in Tokyo many years ago. One warm summer afternoon, I was stopped at the intersection waiting for a walk light. The cars were busily whizzing around like hornets on a hot afternoon. I happened to look up at a billboard-sized electronic sign. Large numerals showed the date, the time, the temperature, and a symbol for the weather forecast (an umbrella indicating rain). But two other numbers especially caught my attention. One indicated the noise level in decibels; the other showed the carbon monoxide level in parts per million. Not surprisingly, when the walk light went on and all the traffic stopped, these two numbers dropped very fast. When the traffic started again, they zoomed upward in response. I thought how political such a sign would be in my own country. There would be environmental groups at every corner with leaflets telling us how we were destroying the environment and what we should do about it. Such a sign would be a call to responsible action.

Yet when I asked some Japanese about the billboard, they seemed quite apathetic. It seemed that the numbers under human control—the noise and carbon monoxide levels—were taken as givens just like the temperature and the weather. Human beings are part of nature and human beings are such a species that they would develop internal combustion engines for transport. According to this line of thought, all the data on the sign were recording "natural" phenomena. There was, in the way we are using the term here, no strong sense of "environmental responsibility" among the Japanese. It seemed to me that, for the Japanese pedestrians, pollution from the automobiles was not much different in kind from the dead trees for the beavers. The question is this: how can we get from this strong sense of intimacy and naturalness to a morally informed ecological agenda? In fact, the Japanese somehow accomplished just that and have been making steady and significant progress in cleaning up their environment, although (like the rest of the industrialized world) they still have a long way to go. How did this change come about?

Although an intimacy-oriented ethics does not, and cannot, require one to be environmentally responsible, it does require one to be ecologically responsive. In destroying nature, human beings are also destroying themselves. We should respond with compassion to the pain of the other species on whom we have imposed our *unnecessary* destructive acts. To know ecological damage is to feel the pain of the earth and to generate a moral impulse to respond. Because humans are part of nature, our ecological destruction is nature's self-destruction. Yet intimacy's ecological ethics also calls on humans to realize that nature's self-healing requires our responsiveness. Because we are part of nature, we can (and sometimes must) be part of nature's revitalization. Humans are to work with nature, as part of nature, in this healing process. We can see the parallel with the aesthetic paradigm in intimacy's orientation. Just as nature expresses itself artistically through the part of nature we call "the artist," nature heals itself through the part of itself known as the "ecologically responsive *Homo sapiens.*"

As an example of how this process might work, consider another anecdote from Japan. Years ago I met a colleague—a philosopher from the southern Japanese island of Kyushu. During one of our conversations, he explained some work he had done for his city as an adviser. One incident he related was particularly relevant to how thinking might proceed in an ethics of intimacy. It happened that in the central part of his city, a large skyscraper had recently been erected and was causing a problem. A small park near the building, a park frequented by mothers and their children from the area, was cut off from sunlight by the new building. A formerly sunny little park had become dark and dingy almost all day long. The flowers were dying and the pool of water was overrun with scum. Mold, mildew, and moss were taking over the rocks and trees. On behalf of the community, the philosopher suggested that the owners of the skyscraper erect a large mirror on top of the building, a rotating mirror that would follow the sun across the sky and reflect its light on the park. Through this device the park was once again the sunny spot that people in the neighborhood had enjoyed. Flowers could grow again. Furthermore, the philosopher recommended that solar panels be placed in the park to catch some of the reflected rays. These solar panels generated electricity to light the park's walkways at night and to run a small pump so that a little waterfall could filter and aerate the water in the park's garden.

For the philosopher, this was not a matter of doing something to penalize the irresponsible action of the developers. It was a matter of acting skillfully as opposed to unskillfully. He was working cooperatively with nature, helping nature's self-healing of a problem nature had caused. Nature had caused that big building to be erected. After all, the people who built it were part of nature as much as the beavers in the previous anecdote. Yet the people could also be responsive to the situation and find a way to help nature heal the wound by using the advanced technologies natural to the human species. The neighborhood people were not set off in opposition to the developers as two independent groups with their own integrity and rights. No attorneys were involved in the negotiation. Rather, the situation was handled by the neighbors and developers as two overlapping groups with a common problem. The solution, an ecologically moral one, arose out of their commonality, not out of a dialectical confrontation of opposing groups.

Let us sum up this section on the ethics toward nonhuman things. We have examined the example of environmentalism and seen that both the integrity and the intimacy orientations can lead to behavior that will protect or improve the environment. The point, however, is that the two orientations would get to the same point by different means of analysis, evaluation, and persuasion. For someone from an intimacy orientation, the talk of environmental "responsibility" or the "rights" of endangered species would not be an effective call to action. For someone from an integrity orientation, conversely, the idea that pollution could be understood as "natural" would be a nonsensical starting point for trying to persuade people to participate in an environmental cleanup. This is a complexity of intercultural and international cooperation on environmental issues. Cultures foregrounding one orientation often have trouble communicating with cultures foregrounding the other orientation. Without shared ground rules of analysis and persuasion, coordinated action is difficult. The lesson is this: there is an important difference between getting cooperation on a specific action and agreeing on a common rationale for the action. Cultures of different orientation might be able to achieve the former, but they are not likely to achieve the latter. If the two cultures use different models of epistemology, analysis, metaphysics, and ethics, they are unlikely to agree on rationales for action. Yet they might be able to arrive at the same conclusion via a radically different route. For the sake of global cooperation, this may be enough. We will return to this issue in the next chapter.

## POLITICS

Politics can be seen as the normative relation among people as mediated by their collectivity instead of their direct interpersonal reactions. Specifically it focuses on the relation between the person and the state or between state and state. In this chapter we will emphasize the former, leaving discussion of the latter to the next chapter. In many respects, the politics of integrity and intimacy are extensions of points already made about ethics.

### Integrity's Version

Because integrity assumes an external relationship among individual persons, each with her or his own integrity, the state is constructed by creating a series of external relations among these discrete individuals. These relations are typically laws that bind the individuals into their political relationships. Integrity tends to see the whole or the state as composed of its parts—its individuals—and the external laws connecting them politically. In other words: the integrity model leads to a conception of the state in terms of *Gesellschaft* rather than *Gemeinschaft*—that is, a society of laws rather than a community of shared identities and overlaps. Through its laws, integrity-based political structures ensure not only cooperation but also inherent protections for the individual's integrity. Specifically, there is often a notion of inalienable rights guaranteeing the preservation of each citizen's integrity. In contexts where the protection of individual rights is particularly emphasized, we find principles maintaining that the state only exists by virtue of, for example, "the consent of the governed" (John Locke) or that government is "of the people, by the people, and for the people" (Abraham Lincoln). The citizens, with their rule-governed relations, constitute the whole.

In such political models, it is not surprising to find sophisticated theories or thought experiments about how the individuals come together to constitute the state—of how the whole is constructed out of the parts and their added external relations. Social philosophers like John Locke and Thomas Hobbes devised social contract theories to do precisely this. In the "state of nature," they argued, there would be no social collectivity of a governmental sort, only discrete individuals without any assumed relationship among them. The social contract establishes the external relations among these individuals—relations that would benefit the whole without completely dissolving the integrity of the individuals.

### Intimacy's Version

In political models growing out of the intimacy orientation, by contrast, we would expect to find theories regarding the members of the state as interdependent so that the state as a whole is holographically reflected in each individual. More like a *Gemeinschaft* model, the state is understood as a logical extension of the overlapping relations of family, tribe, race, and people. If there is a strong structure of hierarchy, the head of the state is understood to be analogous to the head of a family or the head of a tribe and can serve as a primary political holographic reflection of the state as a whole. Conversely, each individual is also in some ways a reflection of the whole as well. Relations between the head of the state and the people are often ritualized in various political praxes. The bonds uniting the people are affective, unreflective, dark, and inexplicable to outsiders, even to a certain extent to the people themselves. Not only were premodern Western versions of monarchy often understood in this way but charismatic leaders often function in this way even in our times outside the monarchic structure. Adolph Hitler, Mao Zedong, Mahatma Gandhi, John F. Kennedy, Fidel Castro—all displayed elements of such leadership. These figures did not merely lead a political movement of individuals sharing a common set of principles; rather, the leader and the members of the movement reflected each other in a holographic way. When Gandhi starved himself in political protest, the Indians of the liberation movement felt his starvation. The people starved with him holographically, some even literally. When the people and the leader are in an intimacy orientation, an attack on the leader only strengthens the people's holographic identification with the leader. This phenomenon may be incomprehensible to a political analyst operating in an integrity orientation. Such an analyst might assume that showing the leader to be weak, vulnerable, or even evil in some sense would lead to a loss of the "people's consent" and an ensuing revolution. That is: such an analyst would think in terms of dissolving the state through destroying the external relation between people and leader. If the state and the people are related internally in an intimacy structure, however, such a strategy targeted at the leader might actually strengthen the leader's holographic character. One could argue that this happened in the failed attempt by Western nations to deal with Ho Chi Minh and Mao Zedong.

The civil function of ritual may be the basis for what is often called "civil religion." Because civil rituals are somatically acquired through the acculturation process, the participants cannot articulate publicly how they feel their commonality and how their roles are reflected in the larger whole. Yet the acculturated participants also have an expert knowledge of how the state is reflected in each individual among them. There are no universal rules defining the respective roles of the state and the individual because this would assume an explicit, external relation between the two. In models of the state operative within the intimacy orientation, one is most fully a member of the state when one practices the ritual forms of the country. Given intimacy's emphasis on somatic praxis, affect, and the nonpublic, therefore, intimacy-dominant cultures and subcultures often emphasize an overlap between church and state. Similarly, the ethnic identity (the being of a people) and political identity (the being of a nation) may also be construed as intimately and inseparably connected.

Another example from Japan may clarify the difference between the integrity and intimacy orientation. When there is a catastrophe such as an airline crash or a public scandal about corporate wrongdoing, it is common practice for the president of the Japanese company to resign—even if there is no clear connection between the individual and the event. From an integrity orientation, it might seem the executive is taking the "ultimate responsibility." That is: as the chief officer of the company, "the buck stops there." If something negative occurs, it can be traced, at least theoretically, to the chain of command ending in the corporate head. In some sense, however abstract, the president must feel responsible for what happened. Yet this is not how the situation is typically understood in Japan. For a culture in which integrity is usually background and intimacy is foreground, "responsibility" is not the salient concept. Rather, the holographic sense of identity means that the corporation is present in each individual and vice versa. Thus if we were forced to use the concept of agency (the sine qua non for a sense of responsibility), we would have to say that the agent for the negative event was everyone. Yet, as in a village hierarchy, the head of the village is the holographic center of the whole and must perform the ritual of purification to eradicate the village's pollution from the broken taboo. Hence the president of the corporation, as the ritualistic focal point of the whole, performs the act of purification by resigning. In so doing, everyone holographically participates in the purification.

In accord with an intimacy-dominant orientation, therefore, Japanese often deemphasize the idea of the individuated political responsibility prominent in most integrity-dominant cultures. This is one reason why the Japanese found it difficult to locate responsibility for the atrocities committed by their military during World War II. By the holographic model, everyone shared the blame. If one had to place blame, it was the emperor, as the focal holographic embodiment of the state, who reflected the guilt of the whole. If this analysis is correct, however, why did General MacArthur's army of occupation not force the emperor to abdicate his throne? Probably because the occupation's command had decided to use the emperor's holographic power as a force for pacification and reconstruction. By controlling rather than dethroning the emperor, one could change holographically the entire state. The occupation, therefore, deflected legal and political responsibility to the long list of "war criminals" subsequently tried and convicted. By controlling the emperor, the occupation forces kept intact the intimacy-based power structure in Japan and through the war crimes trials gave the West a sense of an integrity-based system of responsibility, justice, and sanctions.

The reference to the Japanese emperor suggests something further about intimacy's models of the state. Perhaps because of their emphasis on the somatic, intimacy-dominant models often see the state itself as a single body. The Japanese emperor, for example, is sometimes called the *kokutai*—literally, the "body of the country." This is not a mere metaphor. As recently as the 1980s, people debated whether the Japanese emperor could undergo surgery. What, the people in charge of imperial affairs wondered, would be the implications of cutting open the "body of the country"? In such an intimacy-dominated context, much of the political activity is ritually focused on and through the king or emperor. The monarch is the central holographic image of the whole country. Indeed, monarchs around the world have often been viewed as the "head" of the state, giving it direction that is then enacted by the entire "body politic." By establishing an intimate relation with the state, the individual's significance is never dissociated from the state as a whole. Nor is the identity of the state ever completely dissociated from every individual in it. This analysis points out, by the way, the error in treating this holographic function as a mere trope—a metonym in which the part signifies the whole (as in the locution "the *crown's* authority"). In an intimacy orientation the identification is ontological, epistemological, and normative, not just a figure of speech. It functions as a description of the actual, not simply linguistic or ideological, relationship among things.

Discussing the imperial structure of Japan gives us the opportunity to make a further observation: we should not confuse integrity and intimacy with individualism and collectivism (or groupism). Descriptions of Japan as "collectivistic" and the United States as "individualistic" cannot explain, for example, the successful coordination of Americans necessary in defeating Japan in the Pacific theater of World War II. The people of the United States functioned with a sense of will at least as effective as the collective will of the Japanese. So the contrast cannot be made simply in terms of collectivism. Rather, we have to examine how the collectivism is achieved in each case. In an integrity-dominant culture, an appeal is typically made to each individual's sense of duty to a commonly held principle or set of external values that "bind us together." "We are what we are" because we have an allegiance and duty to a clearly and publicly articulated set of political ideals. In a sense, integrity achieves collective cooperation by challenging the individual to look outside the self, to remember the special contract binding us together, and to reaffirm this contract as the basis of our beneficial way of life. Integrity's call to joint activity is therefore a call to the individual to live up to one's contractual agreements—because without this contract life would be, as Thomas Hobbes suggested, "nasty, brutish, and short."

Intimacy, by contrast, uses a very different discourse to urge collective action. The exhortation is generally, first of all, not to go outside the self but to look deeper within—to find the internal relation that holographically reiterates the whole. The appeal is to an affective, dark core of

connectedness that is not publicly analyzed into external contractual principles. (In the militaristic jargon of the war years, this idea in Japan was
often articulated in terms of the *"Yamato damashii,"* the spirit of ancient
Japan in the hearts of all true Japanese.) This can often take the form of
ethnicity—the notion that there is some distinctive spirit which surges
through our bloodline making us intrinsically, not extrinsically, already
part of a whole. In this respect, we have a paradox: if I die for the emperor
(the holographic focal point of both collective and personal meaning), it
can be seen as a sign of self-preservation. It may be true in some sense I
am dying for others or for future members of my collectivity. But in a
deeper, more intimate sense, I am dying for what I myself now am. One
is not sacrificing the self; one is expressing the fullness of the self with all
its overlaps. In this fully developed sense, intimacy appeals as much to the
person as does integrity, but the meaning of this "person" is defined differently in the two orientations. In intimacy's political analysis we can discern clear similarities with the Mahāyāna Buddhist conflation of wisdom
and compassion mentioned earlier in our discussion of ethics. That is: the
compassion (and its acting on behalf of others) arises spontaneously from
one's insight into oneself and reality.

Another dimension of the discourse involved in the exhortation to collective action is integrity's use of compromise as contrasted with intimacy's emphasis on consensus. The words themselves are revealing. The
word "compromise" breaks down into "com-" (together) and "promise"
(from *"prōmissum,"* something promised); a compromise's essential quality is contractual—a common promise to abide dutifully to a set of principles on which we have established agreement. A "consensus," however,
breaks down into "con-" (together) and "sensus" (from *"sentīre,"* to
feel); consensus' essential quality is a collective perception—a common
sense of what we intrinsically share in our internal relatedness. A compromise is a linguistically explicit contract; a consensus is an affectively
sensed knowledge of everyone's position. This has ramifications for the
mode of negotiation.

In order to reach a compromise in an integrity-dominant context, the
individuals involved "put their cards on the table," explicitly stating what
they need or want in some order of priority. Then the focus turns to these
priorities, balancing them in a give-and-take fashion until a final vote con-
firms the compromise. Usually no one gets exactly what she or he wanted
initially. Yet the desire for something rather than nothing—and the trust
that each negotiator will abide by the contract (without the promise there

is no compromise)—is enough to secure the majority vote. In the case of consensus in an intimacy-dominant context, however, the negotiation is fundamentally different. No individual ever lays out publicly what he or she wants because this would signal a separation rather than an overlap with the others. Such separation only gets in the way of the affectively charged sensing of the commonality behind the emergent consensus. The process leading to consensus uses indirect intimation rather than explicitation. Intimation, as we recall, operates like a hint or an insider joke. I negotiate in a consensus mode when I do not publicly reveal my position but speak indirectly so that the other insiders will get it. As noted in chapters 1 and 2, to my intimates I need say nothing to be understood. The trust in such a consensual context is not that everyone will keep to their promises in upholding the agreement. Instead I trust my colleagues to get what I am intimating and not to proceed without factoring in this aspect. I trust that the others will incorporate my intimations into their own selves: because of our overlaps, they make my interests into our interests. Relating this trust to our previous discussion of ethics, I trust them to be *responsive* more than *responsible*. Something explicit is said only after the internally related sensing of common ground is completed (the con-sensus). If the negotiation has progressed as designed, there will then be a formal statement of the final decision with little or no further discussion.

## PATTERNS OF REPLICATION

This discussion of the three normative domains of aesthetics, ethics, and politics has in many respects reiterated the same basic orientations we found in our discussion of epistemology, logic, and metaphysics. There seems to be a strong continuity in form from the descriptive to the prescriptive philosophical models we have explored. As noted in the Introduction, cultures often display a reiteration of simple patterns to form more complex structures. Acculturation proceeds not so much by imparting content as by impressing forms for receiving, organizing, analyzing, and expressing content. Philosophically, the basic reiterative pattern of intimacy or integrity replicates itself into epistemological, analytic, metaphysical, aesthetic, ethical, and political modes of reflection. In either case, one may find it important to distinguish what-is from what-should-be, but how one tends to think about either is quite consistent within

Table 3. Comparison of the Prescriptive Domains of Integrity and Intimacy

| *Integrity* | *Intimacy* |
|---|---|
| **AESTHETICS** | |
| 1. Art as mediating and relating separately existent self and world. | 1. Art as expressive of intrinsic overlap between self and world. |
| 2. Creativity as artistic autonomy; individual freedom of expression. | 2. Creativity as naturalness or spontaneity arising from self and world together. |
| 3. Work of art as "subjective" addition to world. | 3. Of the world as well as in it; the work of art as necessarily "objective" as well as "subjective." |
| 4. Work of art as having own meaning independent of artist's intent or audience's response. | 4. Artist, audience, work of art as inseparably related. |
| **ETHICS** | |
| 1. "Ought" as preserving other's integrity (or rights). | 1. "Ought" as recognizing and preserving overlap with other. |
| 2. Ethical external relation abstracted into universal principles or maxims; discourse of "responsibility." | 2. Situational responsiveness; discourse of "love" or "compassion" or "responsiveness." |
| **POLITICS** | |
| 1. State composed of individuals bound by social contracts. | 1. State holographically (recursively) present in each individual. |
| 2. Emphasis on individual responsibilities and rights. | 2. Emphasis on individuals as intrinsically also the body of the state. |
| 3. Emphasis on compromise bridging opposing poles. | 3. Emphasis on consensus as inherently shared viewpoint. |

each of the orientations. Table 3 summarizes the points made in our discussion of the three main areas of prescriptive discourse. The table suggests that the differences between intimacy and integrity can be quite rigid. What happens when the two orientations contact each other? Is conflict inevitable? Are communication and cooperation possible? Such questions are the focus of the final chapter.

CHAPTER 6

# INTERCULTURAL CONFLICT

## *WHEN INTIMACY AND INTEGRITY COLLIDE*

So far we have said little about the actual nature of reality. We have focused instead on how people tend to think about reality and persuade others of their position. We found two very different answers to a fundamental question: how are things related? Yet in analyzing this question, we have not tried to answer how things are *really* related. Instead, we have tried to find out how people relate things when they analyze them, discuss them, and evaluate them. We have left open the question of whether one way of thinking about relations is better than another. In fact, we have seen that truth itself may be differently understood and expressed in the two orientations of intimacy and integrity.

Along the way, we have also seen that at least some cultures or subcultures seem to foreground one orientation while leaving the other in the shadows. The marginalized orientation and its products are still there (perhaps as countercultures), but they are typically disempowered—especially when culturally important issues are being analyzed, hashed out, and agreed upon. The more authoritative the analysis, the more likely one or the other orientation will supply the rhetorical vehicle or categorical scheme for the discourse. As noted in chapter 1, a major role of culture is to teach us what counts, what is important, what aspects of our experience deserve our closest attention. The answer to the question "what kind of relation is most important?" is not something that epistemology, analysis, argument, metaphysics, aesthetics, ethics, or politics alone can

133

ever answer. Rather, as we have seen, the answer to this question informs these philosophical fields of where to begin and how to proceed.

There is a sense in which the answer to the question "which orientation best captures reality?" is arbitrary. That is: there is no *rational* basis for choosing one answer over the other. In fact the choice will, as we have seen, strongly influence what will count as "rational" for *any* answer to *any* other question from that point on. People cannot answer a question rationally until they have agreed on what rationality itself means. To do this, they must (among other things) operate within an orientation for thinking about how things are related, at least for the issue at hand. Of course, once a culture or subculture establishes the cultural orientation defining rationality, people who use arguments or analyses from within this authorized cultural orientation will be taken to be "rational" or "smart." At least this is true when rationality is what is considered to be intellectually "persuasive" or "rigorous." This sense of rationality is transmitted culturally through childrearing and educational praxis. Those who excel in the powers of "rational persuasion" as defined within the cultural orientation would tend to have a better chance of rising to positions of authority, leadership, and success. This would in turn establish the privileged place of this orientation all the more firmly in the culture. In this way—as depicted in the pictures of the two trees (Figure 1)—a simple pattern is established and reiterated throughout the culture. By using this pattern, the people in the culture can grow new branches in a consistent and predictable way.

Suppose, however, that a person from this culture encounters people from another culture (perhaps even a counterculture within the same community)—one that has taken the other orientation as its pattern for analysis. Although these other people will be similar in some ways, as one gets to know them more deeply they will seem increasingly exotic in that they seem to think a great deal about things that are not very important. Furthermore, judging from the way they think, they will not seem to place a major premium on rational rigor. Such interaction was behind the phenomenon of cross-cultural opacity discussed at the outset in this book. In chapter 1 we noted some difficulties that integrity-oriented Western philosophers encountered in their attempts to appreciate Japanese philosophy, for example.

My general claim is the following. Everyone, regardless of culture or subculture, probably has some aspects of their personal lives that seem closer to the intimacy orientation and others closer to the integrity orientation. (There may, of course, be other cultural orientations apart from these two.) Yet I am also hypothesizing that each culture or subculture tends to foreground one orientation over the other—to make one more dominant or authoritative in most (not necessarily all) contexts. Insofar as culture has as one of its central aims the unification (or at least the cooperation) of a people, it is critical that these people share a basic understanding about relations, analysis, and persuasion. There must be some common ground, some single starting point, for deciding what kinds of analyses are most pertinent, what forms of reasoned persuasion are most effective, and even what kind of rationality is the one we will all use in developing a shared view of self, world, and other. One cannot argue the grounds for argument. A group of people must start somewhere. And this somewhere is at least in part what I am calling the orientations of integrity and intimacy.

If we accept this theory of cultural orientations, one consequence is that two cultures might diverge early in their development over the simple issue of privileging one way or the other in understanding how relations work. Yet because of differences in these initial orientations, a different set of questions might be asked—a different set of problems might develop as having the most urgency for this culture. As we saw in the preceding chapter, for example, the integrity and intimacy orientations tend to develop different forms of ethics, the former emphasizing responsibility and the latter responsiveness. Because ethical behavior is critical to the development of culture, there will be a philosophical focus on the key ethical term—"what is responsibility?" in one culture and "what is responsiveness?" in the other culture. The answers to these initial questions will in turn contain within them the basis for new questions. A specialized terminology will emerge and certain problems will acquire a sense of historical continuity (what might be labeled "tradition"). As the cultures develop, the trajectories of their intellectual traditions, like the branches of the two trees in Figure 1, will likely continue to diverge. Eventually we reach the point where the traditions either become mutually unintelligible or at least so dissimilar in their purposes that it is difficult for people of one culture to understand why something is important to people of the other culture. Of course, they will not be completely unintelligible. To perceive the other to be "different" requires a basic understanding grounded in a shared logic (as discussed in chapters 1 and 3). Otherwise I would have no basis for knowing that I do not understand the other: I have to understand the other well enough to know I am not fully understanding that other. Consider the following example from my own career in Japanese philosophy.

When I first began studying Japanese philosophy, it struck me as enigmatic. Eventually I reached the point of understanding the issues, but I found it difficult to communicate their relevance to my Western colleagues. After a long, friendly conversation with a fellow American or Western European philosopher about some issue in Japanese philosophy, my colleague would typically say something like: "Oh, now I see. This is rather curious, but I'm not sure it is *philosophically* interesting." When I began to translate Japanese philosophical texts into English, I found that certain basic issues in Japanese philosophy (for example, the relation between primordial and acquired enlightenment) could easily require a page or more of explanation. Even when successfully doing so, however, it was as if I had explained an inside joke to an outsider. The outsider finally understood, but he still did not get it. Such an outsider could understand the issue but never could see how it might be important. And when I found myself in the reverse situation, trying to explain Western philosophical problems to a Japanese philosopher, the result was the same. It might take five minutes to explain to the Japanese what is meant by the mind/body problem or the problem of free will and determinism. And even then the Japanese colleague might understand but still not grasp why this problem was considered so central in Western thought. The Japanese just did not get it. The difference between cultural orientations is not so much a matter of miscommunication or lack of translation as it is a mutual lack of "getting the point."

The account given—the theory that at some early starting point two cultures choosing different orientations would diverge and never meet—could be called "The Road Not Taken" explanation. In the Robert Frost poem of this name are the famous lines: "Two roads diverged in a wood, and I — / I took the one less traveled by, / And that has made all the difference." Once a fundamental choice is made, there is no going back. Japan and the West took opposite paths at some (either logical or historical) moment and they have diverged ever since. However satisfying such an account might be, aesthetically as well as historically, it has significant limitations.

Clearly cultures are not monolithic. In fact there are always a variety of subcultures and even countercultures functioning in a society at a given time. And the one controlled by the elite may be dominant. As the authoritative discourse of the elite, it may become the linchpin of such enterprises as the educational system, the topics of scholarship and analysis, and success in what guarantees leadership and power in that culture. Even so, it seems there are always a few marginalized subcultures playing by different rules (and usually losing) in the contest for power. Thus they remain a minority way of thinking for a marginalized group. This multiculturalism has some ramifications, only one of which we will pursue here. When I first started using "intimacy" as a heuristic for understanding Japanese culture, my students, my lecture audiences, my colleagues, and I began noticing that the exposition of intimacy seemed to have striking similarities with what are often called feminist epistemologies. Indeed, intimacy's characteristics seemed to fit "traditional" characteristics often associated with women in modern European and North American constructions of gender. Specifically we find in common such things as reliance on intuition (the grounds of which are dark and cannot be explicated as empirical or principle-laden), the preference for seeing opposites as overlapping rather than as polarized, the importance of affect as related to knowing, even the traditional correlation of women with the body and men with the intellect. For good or ill, this was the traditional way of classifying the social constructions of the female gender in most European and North American contexts. And it also seems to parallel the intimacy orientation as developed here.

As many popular psychological and family therapy books argue today, the practical significance of gender differences can undermine a heterosexual relationship. The husband, for example, may envision the family as a "household." He may therefore think that the goal is to manage interpersonal relations so that family members respect each other's space and property and have a role in the division of labor with negotiated duties and responsibilities. Meanwhile, the wife may be thinking in terms of the family as a "home" of interwoven relations where members are sensitive to what is not explicitly said, where they share a common identity, and where they nurture interdependence. In times of conflict, communication may break down and the husband (in a societal *Gesellschaft* mode) may accuse his wife of "missing the point" whereas the wife (in a communal *Gemeinschaft* role) accuses her husband of "not listening." It is analogous to an environmentalist trying to persuade an ecologist. The disagreement becomes one of difference in cultural orientation as much as a conflict about the issue at stake.

What should be made of this? Could it be that in the modern, patriarchal cultures of the West (especially before the impact of feminism), the dominant orientation for relations correlated with male roles and the marginalized orientation with female roles? Was there a need to have both orientations represented in the most fundamental human relational group—the family—even though one (the male-correlated integrity orientation) was considered dominant and given the most social authority and prestige? As we have noticed in the various examples explored in the previous chapters, the intimacy orientation seems particularly adept at analyzing certain human experiences (love, for example) whereas the integrity orientation is more adept at others (such as rights). Perhaps the culture, like the individual, needs to draw on both orientations. Yet as we have also seen, the two orientations do not readily blend. The two orientations are so basic and so different that they cannot be emphasized equally without a kind of cultural schizophrenia. Therefore, one orientation is foregrounded in a situation; it becomes the norm: the authorized standard for the interpretation about what thinking, relating, and valuing should be. It becomes the formal basis for settling disagreements and for fixing the discourse or rhetoric of persuasion. In a patriarchal society, of course, men would be taught to focus on the dominant orientation and this would leave the other orientation for the women. In this way, the societal structure reinforces the patriarchy by giving the male-defined roles more cultural authority.

If this speculative hypothesis holds up under scrutiny, it would seem that Japanese and modern Western cultures could be mirror-images in this respect. Let us assume, for example, that both Japan and the United States are traditionally patriarchal in the sense that males have dominated the recognized elite. Yet if the dominant relational orientation in one culture (Japan) is intimacy and in the other (America) it is integrity, we might predict that men would associate with the dominant orientation in each case. We have just seen how this may well have been the case in the United States: in analyzing and talking about a matter of importance, men have been traditionally expected to operate out of the integrity orientation. What, then, about Japan? The first part struck me as being fairly obviously true: the intimacy orientation has functioned in a way that lends power and authority to men. Virtually all the intimacy-oriented examples from contemporary Japanese culture appearing in this book reflect how Japanese males typically think, talk, and interact.

The truly intriguing question for testing the hypothesis would be whether Japanese women function more in the integrity orientation. Although this is a complex issue requiring detailed study, there is at least

some prima facie evidence suggesting the affirmative. While men are traditionally forming overlapping relations with their colleagues and business associates, nurturing an identity with the corporation holographically reflected in each of them as individuals, learning through master/
apprenticeship hierarchies, the wife-mother is generally home with the
children. She typically controls the family finances (giving the husband an
allowance out of his salary), makes the key purchasing decisions (when to
buy a new car and what kind), has total management of the children
(which schools, how best to educate them—probably the most critical decisions in parenting children in Japan), and so forth. I know of cases
where the wife has chastised her husband for coming home too early and
not interacting more with his business colleagues at the bar after work. In
such instances, the wife recognizes that socializing often plays a central
role in promotion at work and hence can lead to increased income for the
family. In this light, it might be argued that Japanese homemakers do not
exchange business cards, not only because they are not important enough
to need them in a patriarchal society, but also because their identity is
more autonomous than holographic. The business card—with its corporate logo, department, and corporate position as well as personal name—
defines the salaryman in terms of the organization of which he is holographically a part. In the case of women who care for the home and
family, however, their identity is not strictly defined by their social context. They may, therefore, have more integrity, even more autonomy, as
individuals.

Yet Japanese mothers also use intimacy-oriented modes of childrearing
(forming an interdependence between mother and child, for example).
So it seems that Japanese mothers, whatever autonomy they may have
within the household, also pass on the intimacy orientation to the next
generation. Indeed, since they have almost complete control of childrearing, if the Japanese mothers did not pass on the intimacy orientation to
their children, the process of acculturation would be seriously undermined. It might be fair to say that while all Japanese children are raised
in the intimacy orientation, the usual male line of development is to move
from the family (one intimacy structure) into the workplace (another intimacy structure). For the male, the corporation at work and the wife at
home play the supportive role formerly played by the mother's nurturing
intimacy. The woman who becomes a wife-mother, by contrast, must
leave her own childhood home of intimacy. She breaks with her former
identity to become the wife-mother in her husband's house. This ability

to take personal identity across contexts is, as we have seen in the discussion of ancient Greek philosophy in chapter 1, a characteristic of integrity, and we can surmise that the girl's upbringing trains her to develop enough integrity to make such a move possible. Having experienced two intimate households (her own and her husband's house), such a woman may develop a capacity to abstract general principles and put them into effect—another characteristic of the integrity orientation. As we can see, therefore, the situation in Japan is complicated and deserves a thorough analysis. Our brief comments, however, illustrate two points. First, in analyzing actual societies or communities, we must be alert to both dominant and nondominant modes of orientation. Second, in doing such an analysis, the distinction between intimacy and integrity may highlight certain points that might have otherwise gone unnoticed. The theory of the two orientations has at least a heuristic or hermeneutic value in helping us to learn and interpret.

Another problem with "The Road Not Taken" analysis is that it does not account for profound cultural changes in history. However much the roads may diverge, one can go back or at least cut across to the other path. Perhaps a bully (such as a colonizing empire with a different cultural orientation) comes along and forces you off the road and onto the path the bully wants you to take. Maybe you find your own road too steep, too boring, or too rocky and decide to find the other one in hopes it will be better. In any case, it does seem that cultures can shift orientation. In Western Europe, it appears that in some ways the early and mid-Middle Ages—much of the so-called Dark Ages—might have been more intimacy-oriented than integrity-driven. If this is true, the term "dark" has a special significance. The Dark Ages were "dark" to the Enlightenment's emphasis on integrity's forms of philosophizing. Socially, the *Gemeinschaft* (community) structure was the norm in the medieval period. Politically, the monarchy found its entitlement to rule through religion (the monarch as holograph of God) or ethnicity (the head of the body politic). Epistemologically, the Dark Age thinkers organized knowledge (as Jung pointed out) in alchemical treatises emphasizing the "conjunction" or "marriage" of opposites, the interpenetration of the somatic and the intellectual, and the encoded, intimate language of the "esoteric arts" learned directly from apprenticing oneself to a master. The clerics typically claimed expert knowledge, and there was no easy way to question their authority unless you were one of them. And so forth. If such a capsule summary is fair, then indeed there might well have been a shift in orientation within the West: the Renaissance, the birth of the modern scientific method, and the Reformation signaling a new emphasis on autonomy, external relatedness, contractual bonds, the separation of body from spirit (supporting justification by faith instead of by works), and the separation of intellect from emotion. The "dark" of the Dark Ages was ultimately replaced by the "clear and distinct" rationality culminating in the Enlightenment's ideal of knowledge—the tradition that has remained epistemologically authoritative for the West over the past two or three centuries. (Even here, however, we must be attentive to countercurrents. For example, the nineteenth-century West developed a duality between an intimacy-dominated romanticism and an integrity-dominated positivism. The latter became more authoritative as the century ended, perhaps because of the efficacy of science-based technology.)

These two points—the importance of subcultures within cultures and the possibility of switching orientation—suggest that it might be possible for a society to reverse or at least renegotiate the roles of the orientations. Let us see what would be at stake in such a choice by considering some major advantages and disadvantages of living in either an integrity-dominant society or an intimacy-dominant society. First, in cultures where the integrity orientation is dominant, rights can be articulated and preserved by the legal system. This does not mean, of course, that integrity cultures always in fact protect such rights. Yet if the culture is truly committed to integrity, when such rights are not protected there are rational grounds for protest and culturally persuasive grounds for demanding change. In such a culture, it is reassuring to know that the authoritative discourse ensures that some options cannot be taken away from me—that I have inalienable rights to speak freely, to practice the religion I want, and to participate, either directly or by representation, in any government actions that might affect me. The social and political system even guarantees people the right to criticize the system. Because the principles behind morality and politics are out in the open, they can be argued about, critiqued, changed, or even eliminated through the process of public discussion, disinterested analysis, and compromise. The idea of rights, whether or not there is a "right to privacy" per se, does at least protect people from meddling by the state. I have a right in most circumstances to be left alone. I have the right to challenge the state if it tries to take away my rights because the government exists only by the consent of the governed. The government must recognize and preserve my integrity. Responsibility—whether ethical or political—can be formally identified.

Second, integrity-based cultures are at least in theory tolerant of diversity because of their respect for autonomy and the individual. All people do not have to agree. In fact, integrity may actively advocate and nurture differences. When a pluralism of perspectives is brought to the table for discussion and negotiation, people can feel more confident that every alternative has been explored before making a collective decision. The assumption is that people can get at the truth best if they look at things from a variety of viewpoints. The preference for diversity, compromise, and the adversarial tradition of jurisprudence are all based on this fundamental assumption. Of course, an integrity-oriented society may fail miserably in practice to achieve such toleration and nurture such diversity. My point, however, is that the orientation contains principles and grounds for individuals to criticize the state publicly for failure to abide by its own ideals. "Social justice" can become a cause on behalf of which individuals can argue and then cooperate.

Third, because knowledge is public in its objectivity, it can ideally be accessed by anyone in an integrity-dominant society. There is something like a "right to know" or at least a "right to be able to find out." A culture that emphasizes the basis of knowledge as clear and distinct rather than dark may develop "sunshine laws" making all government proceedings or documents open to public scrutiny. Because it has no expert knowledge that cannot be openly evaluated by everyone, an integrity-based government is not entitled to function in complete secrecy. With such a strong requirement of evidence and proof, the assumption is that an accusation should be backed up with publicly accessible facts. Even when the authorities charge a person with a crime, the citizen is allowed a public day in court to face the purported evidence before a group of one's equals or peers. Moreover, integrity's form of knowledge seeks universal principles. People in integrity-based cultures and subcultures are comfortable with the abstract thinking that gleans hypothetical universal laws from the data. This orientation is central to the theoretical research behind science and certain kinds of technological development. Such an orientation may underpin a general interest in (and often public support for) what is called "basic research" in science, for example, the type of discoveries that can radically change the way we understand the world. Integrity also supports the idea of uncovering general principles about politics, economics, ethics, epistemology, and logic.

And fourth, an integrity culture supports independence, personal expression, individual creativity, and innovation. It is a free market—a free market of ideas as well as material goods. There is an excitement that derives from the unpredictability of social change and shifting values. Because what is true can be tested by the individual, the individual develops a highly refined sense of being able to "think for oneself." People are encouraged to try out new ideas, develop new products, challenge and rethink the past.

Most of these points about integrity-dominant cultures may be quite attractive. Yet a bright idea generally has a dark side as well. If integrity dominates too strongly, certain dangers emerge. Let us consider three of the most obvious problems. First, the fabric of society can easily deteriorate where there is a strong sense of individual autonomy and discreteness along with an emphasis on innovation. The past comes under such radical scrutiny that continuity is lost. Conservatives get left behind and radicals splinter into an array of disconnected groups—even groups of one. There is a danger of anarchy and anomie: the danger of either dissolving all political bonds or of feeling psychologically and socially disconnected. If the relations to the whole can be erased at no cost to the individual, one feels little restraint when it comes to breaking away from everyone else. The loners feel free even to question the principles of morality and social respect that hold together the external relations constituting the society or the state. Clichés abound: "Relationships are a hassle." "It's not *my* problem." "Let them make it on their own the way I did." "Fight the system."

Second, because of its tendency to underplay the role of the somatic and the affective, integrity can lead to an internal dissociation of the self as well if pushed too far. The person is split between the intellectual and the affective/somatic. The person may stop "listening to the body" and lose the ability to read the intimations of another. No longer feeling essentially connected to anything or anyone, one may respond with either uncontrolled depression or fury—either complete detachment from the social world (the loner) or the body (the anorexic) or else the unreflective, unprincipled assertion of brute somaticity in its most violent form (the rapist or serial killer).

Third, the criteria for public objective knowledge may become so rarefied and so detached from ordinary knowing that a radical relativism is born. With the subordination or repression of intimacy's expert knowledge acquired through somatic praxis and experience, integrity's extreme manifestation may reject elders as having no valuable knowledge. Tradition not only loses its value, but the culture or subculture loses the trust between generations by which tradition is transmitted. Furthermore, if integrity takes the bifurcation between subjective and objective to the extreme, one may completely dominate the other. If the objective stands alone, the affective sense of connectedness—the capacity to feel love or compassion—is lost. If subjectivity completely overtakes objectivity, the claim may be made that because each person's experience is so different— so embedded in politics, personal biography, class, race, and gender construction—public objectivity is an impossible ideal, a mere ruse concocted by the elites to hold onto their power base. In other words: as diversity and individualism get pushed to the extreme, the assumed basis for commonality and objectivity disappears. And if objectivity is impossible, there is only subjectivity. Everyone insists that their values come from their own experience; those without this experience can never understand. The right to freedom of expression and the right to access to knowledge get distorted into a newfound right to believe whatever one wants. The epistemological correlate to political anarchy is solipsism; the psychological form of social anomie is detached aestheticism.

Having made those cautionary remarks about the potential dangers facing cultures or subcultures that foreground integrity too strongly, let us now turn to the advantages and disadvantages of a culture emphasizing intimacy. Again let us begin with the positive ramifications. First, in the ideal intimacy-dominant culture there is a low level of stress insofar as there is a strong sense of harmony with others, a background of common experience, and an interconnectedness with the natural world. One is never alone; there are always the interpersonal overlaps sharing in one's successes and difficulties, one's joy and despair. Even the natural world is intimately related to each person in a way that creates a continually shared, mutual openness. There is a strong safety net—both emotionally and socioeconomically—because it is in the self-interest of those who overlap with you to be responsive to your situation. In one's interdependent connections—not in the ego—lies one's primary source of meaning and value: "your problems are our problems." People will take the time to increase the intimate ties allowing them to read your most subtle intimations. You will not have to explain yourself repeatedly because those close to you (and there are many of them) will know you without your having to speak too explicitly or openly. This, of course, is the ideal. Although intimacy-dominant cultures may not live up to their ideals, there are persuasive, rational ways of arguing that the society or other people are not being "responsive."

Second, in a culture with a strong orientation toward intimacy there is little confrontation and consequently little of the accompanying ego building—the mentality of "watching out for number one." The interdependent web of connections knows each person in the group well enough that a consensus will be quietly reached without adversarial confrontation and direct argument. The members of the group know each other's position even when it is not explicitly voiced. Everyone holographically reflects the whole and takes care of the whole just as the whole takes care of them. Each person is vigilant in monitoring the well-being of the group, and it is everyone's business to neutralize interpersonal conflicts. Because the whole is reflected in each member who is part of it, each individual feels the pain if the group is not harmonious.

And third, aggression is muted in the place where one belongs. Because being part of the whole is intrinsic to one's identity, to turn against any other part of the whole is to turn against a part of oneself. There is no need for detailed rules and retributive sanctions. The prospect of ostracization is enough to keep most people from deviating far from the social harmony—a harmony that they themselves reflect, a harmony that helps establish personal identity, a harmony from which they continually benefit. To go against the group is to distance oneself from these benefits. To rock the boat makes all the passengers seasick, even oneself.

Despite these striking advantages, there can also be, as in the case of integrity, a negative side as well. If intimacy is too strongly emphasized, what might be its negative effects? Let us start with the model of intimate knowledge. Insofar as intimacy privileges a form of knowledge that is unsaid, intuitive, and cannot be shared with nonexperts, it is difficult, maybe impossible, for an outsider to analyze and challenge this knowledge. Criticism from an outsider is, by definition, criticism from someone who does not know, from someone who "does not get it" or "is not listening." This is comparable to the way an outsider is not positioned to judge whether an insider joke is funny. To criticize from the inside is not much easier, however. In fact, if an apparent insider criticizes the group consensus, some might begin to wonder aloud whether this person is truly an insider, truly "one of us." Unless deftly done, criticism by an insider can be

considered betrayal of the group and grounds for ostracization. To be ostracized from the intimate circle amounts, as we have seen, to losing
interconnections defining personal identity. With such an extraordinary
power to destroy a person—as "person" is understood in this orientation—the stakes in going against the group are very high. Because non-
confrontation may seem wiser than risking ostracization, the consensus
may degenerate into a forced consensus typified by silence and the threat
of exclusion from the insider group. This points to a difference between
intimacy's necessity for consensus versus integrity's mere possibility for
unanimity.

Because they are superficially cognate ideas from two different orientations, we should be clear about the distinction between consensus and
unanimity. Unanimity assumes a voting process in which each person
votes one's own position, opinion, or conscience. To this extent it preserves the integrity of the individual, and the collectivity of individuals
constitutes the decision-making process. Furthermore, for integrity's
decision-making process it is acceptable if unanimity is never reached so
long as those in the minority position agree to comply with the vote of
the majority. Hence we have integrity's ideal of the "loyal opposition" or
the "loyal minority," a contractual agreement that allows the voicing of
individual difference but still assures cooperation. Consensus, by contrast,
occurs when each person formulates their own opinion in light of the
group as a whole—a holographic mode of relation. Consensus involves a
process in which there is no vote per se or only, as it were, the one vote
of the unified whole. The agent in a consensus is the unified group, not
the individuals in the group, and the individual vote is replaced by the
holographic reflection of the whole in each individual. To reach a consensus, therefore, the decision-making process (the persuasive rhetoric) ideally adjusts both the holograph and the individuals until it achieves the recursive dynamic of the whole-in-parts.

When consensus works well, it gives the group and individuals a strong
sense of common purpose. It does have the disadvantage, however, of
being potentially a powerful form of coercion on the individual who dis-
agrees with the emergent consensus. The only way for the individual to
assert one's difference is to ostracize oneself from the group. (In traditional Japan, this self-ostracization was sometimes expressed in the
protest of ritual suicide: seppuku.) As a Japanese proverb pithily states the
issue: the nail that sticks out gets hammered first. For a consensus to be
reached, it is best if the individuals come to the decision-making process

without a preformed opinion. That is: the process works best if one comes to it with no individual point of view but rather an attitude of openness that seeks to be sensitive to the emergent consensus opinion. Those who bring this inchoate responsiveness do not have to give up their own initial position. No one loses face. Yet given this structure, the opposing points of view are less likely ever to be voiced. In fact, they may not even be formulated in any individual's mind. In this model, there can be no "loyal opposition" or "loyal minority." By definition, the "minority" is not "of the whole" and so a "loyal minority" is an oxymoron.

In short, then, intimacy may place an extraordinary amount of power in the hands of the select. Furthermore, by the authority vested in expert and insider knowledge, the select are necessarily in some respects self-selected. When the system is working well, this is not a difficulty. There is nothing wrong in having gymnastic events judged by experts who have a nonpublicly verifiable knowledge, for example. Yet would we want such judges to determine innocence and guilt in a criminal trial? Should criminality be left to the determination of a small group of "experts" who act out of an intuition that cannot be justified to others? Should a cadre of experts have sole authority over a country's national policy, international relations, or economic stability without being accountable to the people? Insofar as intimacy's leaders, the select, are those with the most "dark" esoteric knowledge that cannot be made public, there is again the danger of there being no standpoint from which to oppose a decision purported to be of the whole.

A second negative aspect lies in intimacy's holographic model itself. Its emphasis on interpenetration can, as we have noted, lend a sense of security in some respects. But we should also note that its structure is inherently totalitarian. Because the whole is in each person, the whole interacts with the person intimately in all sorts of ways. A holographic model of the state tends to provide all the necessary social safety nets (for health, employment, education, retirement, social services, and so forth). Yet if the intimacy becomes too strong, the state can control, not merely supply, these services. Only certain books can be taught, only certain ideas can be written or spoken, and so forth—all in the name of building a base of common experience and knowledge on which one can form a social consensus. The experts know best how to train future experts, and the people are expected to accept their authority. If combined with a particularly strong emphasis on the country's being run by a group with expert knowledge—a group that cannot in practice be effectively criticized—the foundation for a malevolent totalitarianism is in place. If the integrity model gone wild may lead to anarchy, social dissolution, and anomie, the intimacy model gone wild may lead to fascism.

A final danger lies in the powerful role of the "we"—insiders to the circle of intimacy. The problem is in defining the expanse of the circle. A family, a club, a group of graduates from the same college, a political lobby, a church, and so forth may constitute intimacy groups. But how large might the largest functional circle of inclusiveness be? Intimacy groups often draw a sharp line between "us" and "them"—between "insiders" and "outsiders." That is: intimacy defines the internal relations among "us," but those outside our circle are not internally related to us in any important sense. Intimacy groups, paradoxically, may feel protective of the "integrity" of their "intimate circle," limiting access to outsiders. If the largest intimacy circle is restricted to a national or ethnic group and does not extend to humanity (or even the planet) at large, for example, intimacy may supply a rationale for excluding certain other groups from all domains of discourse: moral, political, aesthetic, and authoritative (the realm of "expert knowledge"). This is particularly dangerous because, as we have seen, the intimacy orientation does not tend to generate universal principles. Therefore, the realities and values of the intimacy group tend not to extend beyond the group. "Outsiders" are not only excluded from the "we," but the intimate "we" has no human relationship with them at all. The outsiders become quite literally "nonpersons."

The danger of seeing outsiders as nonpersons is removed, by the way, if an intimacy society takes pains to include "humanity" as a circle of intimacy holographically present in each human being. Although this sense of belonging *with* all humanity is conceptually very different from integrity's idea of rights, the two may be functionally or pragmatically almost equivalent. Such an identification with everyone—of all humanity as being part of what one oneself is—can be (as we saw in the previous chapter) the basis for a responsive ethics of compassion. Without this shared identity with all humanity, however, the intimacy-driven society can readily fall prey to the rational justification of racism, ethnocentrism, sexism, class elitism, or jingoism. And, as we have seen, if intimacy is too strongly foregrounded in such a society, it is difficult to criticize the society effectively. Therefore, intimacy often blurs differences within itself while sharpening the separation from outsiders. I once heard a Japanese scholar say, for instance, "Unlike you Westerners, we Japanese are not dualistic." Since his very distinction was dualistic, what could he possibly have meant? We can make sense of his statement if we assume that when he was interacting with Japanese in a circle of intimacy, he was not dualistic; but he was sharply dualistic in how he viewed those inside and outside the circle. This example signals the crucial importance of where the lines of intimate circles are drawn. As we noted earlier, when intimacy's circle is demarcated rigidly the people will protect the circle's integrity from invasion by outsiders. This can become a paradox, for example, for a feminist group that excludes male membership while professing "inclusiveness" and nonbinary thinking as its primary values.

So where should we turn? Assuming that the foregrounding and backgrounding of the intimacy and integrity paradigms can be switched, would it make sense, for example, for Japan to become an integrity-dominant culture or for the Western countries to become intimacy-dominant? It is possible to envision such an extreme shift, but it is not likely and may not even be prudent. To make such a fundamental shift in orientation is to challenge the foundations of knowing and valuing. Such shifts seem to have occurred before (in the transition from the medieval West to the modern West, for example, as suggested earlier), but such an upheaval is always risky. This is especially so in today's context when humanity has acquired the know-how to destroy with such awesome efficiency. In such circumstances, it is dangerous to undermine the accepted rules of rational discourse and persuasion.

Consider, for example, the case of the former Soviet Union. It had established essentially an intimacy-based political structure with its republics and satellite states. That is: the USSR established a forced consensus that unified the states, not into a federation that preserved the voting rights of the individual states, but rather a union (made up of "comrades" not citizens) under central control. Decisions made by those with expert knowledge (the Politburo) were theoretically reflected in each individual holographically. If there was dissent, this implied the dissenter was not part of the whole and needed to be ostracized (the Gulag) or "reeducated" into the communist consciousness. If former nation-states wished to establish autonomy, this was proof that "the revolution was not yet complete" and military intervention was needed. The Communist Party was not a political "party" in the liberal democratic (integrity-based) sense—there was theoretically no opposition against which the party could be partisan. Instead the party represented a hierarchical holographic system used to distinguish insiders from outsiders—that is, the "bourgeois imperialist, capitalist states." When the internal relations characteristic of the Soviet Union dissolved, independence movements erupted throughout Eastern Europe and Central Asia. Various substates of the USSR and Yugoslavia demanded autonomy: recognition of their political integrity and rights against the totalitarian holism of the former system. Yet they still retained intimacy-based notions of ethnic (and religious) purity. Thus the processes of inclusion and exclusion ("ethnic cleansing") were violently enforced with the consequence of enormous human suffering. Perhaps some time in the future the groups will learn to recognize their mutual internal relationships beyond their ethnic identities or perhaps they will collectively contract into an integrity-based state guaranteeing rights to all, but in the meantime there is violence and chaos without common grounds for agreement or negotiation. Such an example shows the inherent hazards of changing too quickly the orientation that has created political stability and peace up to now. In a nuclear age such upheavals are all the more problematic.

It is perhaps not prudent, then, to advocate radical shifts in orientation. Another obvious alternative is to do nothing: to recognize the difficulties and try to live with them, softening them whenever we can. There would still remain, however, conflicts between the cultures (or subcultures within a single society) emphasizing different orientations. It is worth pausing to think about what happens when an intimacy culture and an integrity culture try to cooperate or even merge. The most obvious problem is also the most ineluctable: what kind of relationship can be established between two cultures having a deep commitment to different paradigms of relationship? That is: which kind of relationship will orient the interaction between the two kinds of relation? Is the relationship between intimacy and integrity to be characterized as one of intimacy or one of integrity?

In international affairs today, worldwide organizations such as the United Nations or the World Bank aim to achieve global cooperation on the basis of a proposed integrity orientation with its rules, contracts (such as trade agreements), and sanctions. But what does this entail for countries operating mainly with an intimacy orientation? Such a proposal requires them to alter the fundamental way of understanding relationship itself. To change the orientation in politics involves, as we have seen, basic changes in epistemology, analysis or persuasive rhetoric, metaphysics, ethics, and even aesthetics. Without making these further changes, how could the intimacy-dominant nation understand and value what the integrity-dominated nations mean, intend, and want? How could such a nation reason persuasively with them over points of contention? To be persuasive, it has to relinquish the very basis of authoritative discourse in its own cultural orientation, the orientation it is trying to preserve. How could it have a shared view of reality and value as a basis for dialogue with the integrity-dominant discourse of the other nations? How could it even agree on values, including the ethical values at the basis of any trusting interaction? In short: to suggest that global cooperation should be grounded on integrity actually involves a suggestion that people from intimacy-dominant cultures should change their fundamental way of viewing themselves, their world, and their values. It is not a simple matter of saying: "You may continue going about doing things as you have always done, but just change this *one thing* in your society" (just recognize the inalienable nature of human rights, for example). Such a change —if it were to be a real change and not superficial playacting—would involve a change in the fundamental cultural orientation within which an intimacy-dominated society constructs meaning. It would entail changing the fundamental reiterative patterns of the culture. Thus it is not really a matter of changing one thing; it is a matter of changing *everything*.

Unless humanity does something, such struggles for authority and for control of discourse between cultural orientations will persist. Without privileging one orientation over the other, however, there is no way even to analyze or argue, let alone resolve, the conflict. If such cultural collisions are taking place not only between cultures but also between subcultures within single societies (such as the gendered subcultures mentioned earlier as well as possibly other subcultures involving class, race, economic status, and religion), it seems that the increasing recognition of cultural plurality and diversity will lead to even further irresolvable conflicts. The difficulty is that harmony and cooperation depend on mutual trust; trust in turn depends on relationships; and the dominant models of relationship are different in the two orientations. It is hard to maintain a relationship, to do the negotiating necessary to keep it alive, if what counts as truth, what counts as knowledge, and what counts as value are not only different but arrived at through different lines of analysis. The cognitive dissonance shuts down the relation building.

Clearly another plan is needed. Somehow one must meld the two orientations in a way that can be tolerated and used by both sides in the cutural collision. (Indeed this would seem the natural approach in an intimacy orientation that seeks to reject bipolar alternatives and build a consensus out of the overlap of opposites.) How can this come to pass? How can one meld two systems that appear to be mutually exclusive? One option—perhaps the simplest—is to divide all relations into two kinds: those of intimacy and those of integrity. In fact, human beings seem to need both orientations and in everyday life people probably alternate between them. My relation with my bank is most likely founded on integrity and contract whereas my relation with my children is most likely based on intimacy and love. Yet how can one know when to operate out of which orientation? If I divide my relationships into two groups, what is the relationship between the intimacy and the integrity groups? What if the people with whom I want to cooperate do not agree with me on how to make the divisions? Is the relationship between intimacy and integrity internal or external? Because of this difficulty, it seems necessary that on some fundamental level we must give priority to one orientation over the other. If this priority is necessary on even the personal level, it is easy to envision how one orientation can predominate over the other in a culture.

There is a deeper problem with the idea that somehow I can oscillate between integrity and intimacy—that sometimes I accept the intimacy orientation and sometimes the integrity orientation. The problem is that I might well want to say that some things about relations are always true. If I accept the notion of universal human rights (an idea emerging from an integrity orientation), for example, what would such rights amount to if I oscillate between having them and not having them? That is: if I swing back and forth between one orientation that recognizes universal human rights and another that does not, the very idea of universal rights is undermined. Simply put: I cannot sometimes have and sometimes not have an innate, inalienable right, yet this is what the oscillation alternative would seem to entail. Insofar as it does, such oscillation indirectly sides with intimacy over integrity. So it does not really solve the problem of balancing the two at all.

Fortunately, there seems to be another alternative. In this book we have periodically noted the common philosophical error of thinking that what we can cognitively distinguish must exist as distinct entities. As we noted in chapter 4, Aristotle showed Plato was wrong in thinking that if we can distinguish form from matter, then form and matter must exist independently. Perhaps in characterizing the oscillation alternative, we made a similar sort of error. That is: just because integrity can recognize universal human rights does not imply that universal human rights exist as a discrete reality. Conversely, just because intimacy cannot recognize such rights does not mean they do not exist. What if we understand intimacy and integrity as a way of working with concepts and values but make no claim that either orientation tells us what reality actually is? Perhaps reality, values, and relationships can be discussed in at least two radically different ways. The orientations describe not reality but rather the way groups of people (cultures or subcultures) interact with each other conceptually, axiologically, and relationally. Then the cultural orientation tells not what reality is, but how people function culturally in terms of reality. If one accepts this view, then one can recognize that my people in our cultural orientation interact and analyze things in one way, but people in other cultural orientations may interact and analyze things in another way. So long as people of a single culture or subculture can communicate well with each other, can analyze persuasively according to accepted modes of authority, and can establish relations of trust, their cultural orientation is effective. Yet in the approach developing here, both cultural groups would accept the idea that although "we" think and talk about things in one way, this does not mean that our orientation exhausts (or even has privileged access to) the nature of reality.

If we follow this suggestion, integrity and intimacy begin to resemble two different natural languages. As Germans talk to each other in German and Britons in English, for example, in one culture people may analyze and communicate with each other in the integrity orientation and in another in an intimacy orientation. Yet just because the German language distinguishes the genders of nouns, this does not mean that every noun refers to an item in reality that actually has gender. To think of the words for chairs, cliffs, and cloth as being masculine, feminine, or neuter does not suggest that the referents themselves actually have these genders. In speaking German with other German-speakers, however, one must make these distinctions. So one does. But one does not presume that what is required by speaking the language necessarily corresponds with the way reality is configured.

Analogously, when in a circle of intimacy it makes sense to interact within the intimacy orientation; and when in a context of integrity, to interact in that orientation. One can shift between the two because one knows neither is the only rational way of portraying reality, knowledge, and value. As a bilingual German- and English-speaker moves back and forth between the languages befitting the audience, so too can one be culturally bi-orientational in thinking and valuing. When speaking German, all mentioned things are gendered; when speaking English, they are not. When operating in an intimacy orientation, relations are primarily internal; when in an integrity orientation, they are primarily external. We do not assume that reality itself changes when we switch languages, so why should we think reality changes when we shift orientations? In both cases, what changes is the way we deal with reality, not reality itself. We change languages or orientations in order to change the group of people with whom we interact.

Although we may seem to have returned to the oscillation model of going back and forth between the two orientations, in fact we have added a new dimension of reflectivity. That is: we may not only use the orientations, but we are now aware of them as simply orientations. We accept that their authoritative or persuasive force is internal to the cultural orientation. The culturally oriented forms of knowing and valuing cannot transcend the orientation and situate authoritative reasoning outside the orientation. Note, however, that if one is bilingual, one does not alternate one's words between German and English. When a person speaks one language, he or she speaks only that one, submitting to its rules of syntax, semantics, and pragmatics. In the same way, when acting from the intimacy orientation, one should not mix this interaction with integrity relations (and vice versa). No one can operate within an orientation of internal relations and simply add on the idea of universal human rights, for example. Yet this does not mean that one has to believe only one orientation captures reality as it is (that rights either exist or do not exist in an ontological sense, for example)—any more than one would think German or English is the only language for speaking the truth.

In a sense, a consequence of this view is that the "metaphysics" in either orientation is understood to be only a form of discourse for interacting with interlocutors of the same orientation. Does this not, once again, favor the intimacy orientation over the integrity orientation? That is: we have seen that the integrity orientation tends to think of truth in terms of the "correspondence" between the idea (or statement) and the reality. If we reduce metaphysics to being a form of discourse and analysis—rather than a set of statements corresponding to an externally related reality— have we not cut the legs out from the entire integrity system? Not really. In claiming that the integrity orientation is not the only way of capturing reality, we have not denied that it is *one* legitimate, rational way of doing so. The integrity and intimacy orientations, as noted in chapter 1 when we discussed the gestalt pictures, are takes on what-is. In the picture of the old woman/young woman (Figure 5), for example, it is true from one take to say it is a young woman but equally true from another that it is an old woman. This does not leave us with a radical relativism in which any interpretation is as good as any other, however. In *neither* gestalt, for example, is it correct to say the woman (young or old) is looking over her left shoulder. The young woman is looking over her right shoulder; the old woman is looking downward with her chin on her chest. If one were asked, however, whether the woman is looking over her shoulder or looking down, the answer would depend on the orientation of the questioner. Although one could say "either or both," it is generally more efficacious to determine the orientation of the question and answer accordingly. The woman who is looking down is not the same as the woman who is looking over her shoulder. This is analogous to responding in either (but not both) German or English depending on the language of the inquirer.

This solution to the problem of negotiating the two orientations may seem simple, but it has important consequences. If I ask whether there are *really* innate human rights in every individual, for example, the answer is indeterminate until there is an orientation within which the terms assume meaning. It is not correct, by the way, to simply say "yes and no" or "there are such rights from one perspective, but not another." Just as we must give our answer in one particular language, we must answer in any given moment from one or the other cultural orientation. There is no meta-orientation to talk about orientations. (If there were, one would have to state how the orientations and meta-orientation relate and in so doing commit to one or the other orientation.) There is no transorientational take on the two orientations. To talk about the relationship between the two orientations is to favor one orientation or the other. Thus people do not simultaneously have and not have human rights. Nor do they sometimes have and sometimes not have human rights. Nor do rights exist or not exist independently of our orientation. Just as all of these statements are themselves in one language or another, any statement about the possibility of the two orientations must itself be uttered in one orientation or the other.

Again our gestalt picture of the young woman/old woman is helpful. If the take is of the old woman, there is nothing one can say about the "the woman's left ear." But if the take is of the young woman, one has a fairly good view from which to make an analysis. Alternatively, if one wants to talk about "the woman's mouth" one can only do so from the gestalt of the old woman. So what a person can analyze—what one can point out to others in discursive acts of persuasion—depends on the take.

Analogously, a concept like human rights can be persuasively discussed in one orientation but not another.

The young woman/old woman gestalt also illustrates why the tack we are taking does not lead to simple perspectivalism. Perspectivalism—the theory that reality can only be seen or described from one perspective at a time and so the characterization of reality depends on the perspective one takes—allows the possibility of complementarity. If you see the table from the top and I from the bottom, for example, we can put our two descriptions together to form a "fuller" description. There is the familiar Indian story of the blind men and the elephant. Each is allowed to touch the elephant and from this evidence describe what an elephant is like. The man who feels the tail says an elephant is like a whip; the one who feels the trunk says it is like a snake; the one who feels the leg says it is like a tree trunk. From the standpoint of perspectivalism, however, once they learned they felt different parts of the same animal, they could collaborate to give a more accurate description of the beast.

There is an important sense, however, in which the two takes in the gestalt picture do not parallel the men's descriptions of the elephant. Are the two takes in fact perspectives on part of the whole picture? No, they are takes on the *whole* picture itself. A person whose take is that of the young woman could never persuade the person whose take is that of the old woman about the nature of, for example, the "woman's left ear." The response of the second person would be more consternation than persuasion: "the other person is trying to persuade me about something for which there is no relevant information, no basis for analysis." If the second person could indeed be persuaded to consider the woman's left ear, this would require an entire shift in gestalt. That is: it would require an entirely different take on reality, on what there is and how to analyze it. This is the contradiction when, for example, an integrity-dominant culture asks an intimacy-dominant culture to "stay the same" but "just add one thing—the idea of human rights."

In sum, then, it seems that the best alternative, as individuals and groups, is to make ourselves culturally bi-orientational—similar to the way people can be bilingual. That is: if we acculturate ourselves to both orientations, both may become more or less second nature to us. If this happens, we would be able to move fluidly between them depending on whom we are with. Intimacy and integrity are different enough that we may never be fully successful in balancing the two—as with languages, one may be my "native" cultural orientation and the other my "second" orientation. Still, the better we can adjust the way we analyze and communicate, the more successful we will be in establishing fruitful, pragmatic, and effective relations with a diversity of others. There is something we will have to give up, however—namely, the idea that there is only one legitimate take on reality. This kind of dogmatism will have to go. If our temperament is to be argumentative or dogmatic, we can still be that way—but only within the parameters of the cultural orientation we are currently taking. I can argue all I want about the young woman or the old woman, but I cannot argue that one is the "reality" and the other the "projection." I cannot argue orientations; I can only argue within them.

This does not mean, however, that I have to give up my values, goals, or ideals—only that I must be willing to analyze them or argue about them in different orientations. Assuming Japan is a culture in which the intimacy orientation still predominates, if I want to convince Japanese they should stop killing whales, it is not persuasive in the long run to pose my argument in terms of "animal rights" or "our ethical responsibility" to be "stewards of nature." This would be like talking about the left ear of the woman to someone who only sees the old woman. Instead, it might be more persuasive to talk in terms of being "responsive" to ecological factors of which we are a part, to feel "compassion" for destroying the whales' "intimate" relations with their families and natural surroundings, to show how "their suffering" is "our suffering." If we do not make such an orientational adjustment in our analysis, it is as futile as arguing in German with someone who knows only French. It is not so much a matter of changing what we believe as it is a matter of changing how we talk about it. Such reflections shed further light on the idea of "cultural philosophy" discussed in chapter 1. Philosophical argument is always cultural insofar as it proceeds within a cultural orientation. We do not argue philosophy; we argue *in* or *through* philosophy. This insight into the cultural nature of philosophy derives from our exploration of the philosophy of culture.

In closing, I should comment on the overall cultural orientation of this book. A reflective reader may accuse me of a kind of hypocrisy. Although I may speak of being bi-orientational, the orientation of analysis and argument in this book is quite one-sided—skewed toward integrity in my attempt at a persuasive, authoritative discourse. Indeed, to the extent the basic thrust of the book is to distinguish integrity and intimacy as discrete, incompatible forms of orientation, the rhetoric is undeniably couched in an integrity mode. It defines the two orientations in a bipolar way and discusses each as having, as it were, its own integrity. This decision to foreground one orientation in discussing the two orientations was unavoidable, however. Trying to make a philosophical analysis without adopting a cultural orientation is like trying to make a pun that is not in any language. The discourse has been in American English (where integrity tends to predominate in scholarly writing). And even when discussing non-Western ideas, it has been formulated largely in modern Western philosophical categories like "ontology," "ethics," and "epistemology" (a context where, again, integrity predominates). So there was an assumption that readers would bring questions primarily from an integrity standpoint.

Could the analysis of the two orientations have been done by foregrounding intimacy? Certainly it could. But then it would, at least initially, have been most persuasive to readers of that cultural orientation rather than the cultural orientation I assumed. What, though, would such an analysis have been like? From intimacy's orientation, intimacy and integrity would overlap. It would be as if the gestalt picture were viewed always as either (*a*) "a gestalt picture that can be either old woman or young woman but which I am going to discuss here as old woman" or (*b*) "a gestalt picture that can be either old woman or young woman but which I am going to discuss here as young woman." That is: the analysis would not begin from poles of intimacy or integrity; rather, the two would emerge out of their overlapping *in medias res*. As with yin and yang, one pole could never exist independently of the other. The balance between the two would contextually shift so that one would sometimes predominate over the other but at other times would be subordinate.

I suppose I could write the book again—this time allowing the intimacy orientation to be foregrounded as a way of analyzing the integrity/intimacy relation. There is a more interesting venue to the same destination, however. As I have been suggesting all along, I believe that Japanese philosophy has historically tended to be intimacy-dominant. This is not a universal claim, just a generalization. There are, of course, exceptions. Indeed there are examples throughout Japanese history when this dominant orientation was challenged by ideas that would be more akin to an integrity orientation—the late-nineteenth-century impact of modern Western philosophy being only the most recent example. The question is how the "mainstream" philosophers of the tradition responded to the situation of recognizing the two orientations when they came into contact with each other at various times. In studying this phenomenon, we will have a historical case study of how at least one intimacy-dominant culture or subculture articulated and analyzed the intimacy/integrity distinction. This study will be the topic of a subsequent book.

As I explained at the end of chapter 6, there is no denying that this book was written from an orientation closer to integrity than intimacy. To write it otherwise would require, in fact, writing a whole new book. To compensate a bit, however, I will conclude with a bibliographic discussion in a mode more oriented to intimacy than integrity. The ensuing discussion is not only our last example of how an intimacy orientation may function. It also suggests how accustomed we have become to bibliographies presented in an integrity-dominant manner, a format that may have some hidden assumptions. Therefore, this intimate bibliography is an experiment in trying to present "sources" as internally, rather than externally, related to this book and its author. For an intimate bibliography, what counts about books is not the integrity of their existence in the Library of Congress Catalog or *Books in Print* but instead their relation to my reading them at a certain time and place of my own personal philosophical development. For an intimate bibliography, the reading of a book, not the book per se, is most relevant. To think of the cited book and this present book as existing independently until "I" connected them is to obscure the overlap among the books. The reading of one book and the writing of another are two aspects of a single event. An intimate bibliography takes the *in medias res* of this event as its point of departure. To explain how the reading of a book is a "source" for this book, therefore, will sometimes lead me to explain people and events related to the context of the reading.

The prospect of thinking about a bibliography in an intimate way opens some fundamental questions about the nature and purpose of bibliographies. There was a time when having a long list of unannotated sources relevant to the book was a laborsaving device for readers. If readers wanted to learn more about the topic, the list of books informed them of what was "out there." This device was particularly valuable since scholars who wrote academic books often had access to specialized library collections and could inform readers about the existence of books that might not be locally available. In today's computer age, this rationale is becoming less compelling. Computer searches of library collections worldwide, on-line bibliographies, and bibliographies associated with websites are making such lists less crucial. In fact, electronic bibliographies have the extra virtue of being able to be infinitely renewed and updated—impossible for a hardcopy list. This does not mean that printed lists are obsolete, but the need for such lists depends a great deal on the subject.

A second reason for an unannotated bibliographic listing is to give full information for footnotes or endnotes. Readers have probably noticed, however, that this book does not use footnotes or endnotes. Since this is becoming quite rare in academic books, an explanation is called for. I first expressed the argument of this book as the 1998 Gilbert Ryle Lectures delivered at Trent University. For that series of lectures, footlights were more appropriate than footnotes. Nor did I conclude my lectures by ritually reciting a bibliography of authorities at the end. Admittedly, since those lectures have transmigrated into the world of literary texts, there is an opportunity—some would say a responsibility—to include the usual scholarly accouterments of notes and standard bibliography. In fact, as I began extensively rewriting and expanding the text of the Ryle Lectures for this book, I started inserting footnotes along the way. After a couple of months, I gave up, however. Part of the problem was that it became an endless task: the book operates at a level of such theoretical generality that almost anything could be relevant. In fact, if the heuristic has any virtue at all, it is precisely in its capacity to address a wide variety of issues and contexts. Notes tended to pigeonhole, rather than open up, the text in the way I wanted.

Another reason for avoiding notes and the ordinary kind of bibliography in this book is that it is a thought experiment—a thinking through of a few premises to understand their consequences. To footnote a thought experiment is akin to footnoting a poem. There is a story that Robert Frost was once asked why he did not footnote his poems as T. S. Eliot had done in "The Wasteland." Frost reportedly replied that one day he had started footnoting "Stopping by Woods on a Snowy Evening," but gave up less than halfway through, having already accumulated more than ten pages of notes for the sixteen-line poem. In a related vein, my uneasiness about having the customary footnotes and bibliography in a book such as this reflects an aspect of my own philosophical training. When I started studying philosophy in the late 1960s and early 1970s, the philosophical books we read seldom had footnotes, except perhaps to give the location of a quoted or cited passage. (Although we rightly credit an individual's *articulation* of an idea, the idea itself—as I will be showing in this intimate bibliography—is often so embedded in a complex social web that it is nigh impossible to speak definitively of "origins.") I remember as a graduate student being surprised to learn there were professional journals of philosophy explicitly forbidding footnotes or endnotes. The point, we were told, is that a philosophical position stands or falls on its own merits and, for this concern, it is basically irrelevant who said what first. If my teachers had had the technical term available to them, they might have expressed this as follows: "A philosophical argument is expected to have its own integrity."

To trace an idea back to its source is a valuable historical enterprise; it can illuminate the sociological and cultural history of knowledge, including its structures of organization and authority. Yet our mentors admonished us not to collapse the history of philosophy (which studies ideas as having *causes* arising in a certain time and place) and constructive or critical philosophizing (which examines whether there is a good *reason* for holding a particular position regardless of its historical cause). To understand the philosophical heritage of a culture—to examine whence ideas arose and how they were formulated—footnotes add valuable context and evidence. To make or engage a philosophical argument, however, notes are not so useful and may even be a distraction. Social scientists may be comfortable appending a "list of authorities" to the end of their texts, but we learned that the philosopher was supposed to question not only the constructs in the authoritative texts but also the criteria by which they gained such authoritative status. Furthermore, once I started studying non-Western traditions, I realized that the closer one stays to historical precedents in philosophizing about a problem, the more difficult it is to question assumptions behind the traditional formulation of the problem itself.

Of course, a bibliography may be something other than a simple list of relevant works. It can be a way of setting the context of a project. No work is born in a vacuum. Writers owe it to their predecessors and successors to define the playing field on which this particular language game has been played. Yet there is something disturbingly logocentric and bibliomanic about the assumption that books alone, or even books primarily, define this context. Here an extended example may help. In working out the argument for this book, the notion of recursive cultural patterns was helpful to me as I hope it will be helpful to readers. To explain the idea as simply, clearly, and provocatively as possible, I utilized the diagrams of the two trees in the Introduction. This is probably as fundamental a point as any other in the book, but where did it come from? In what womb did this idea come to life? For the purposes of bibliographic citation and for giving credit where it was due, I tried to understand the idea and its sources. Yet the more I thought about it, the more I entered a vast array of overlapping circles of influence. It seems that even a single foundational idea is embedded in an intricate web of interdependence. Fifteen or twenty years ago, I had heard of recursive sets, but the idea gained concreteness for me when I purchased a software package called, as I remember, "Stupid PC Tricks." (The title derives from David Letterman's "Stupid Dog Tricks" in his nightly television show.) The package included a program for exploring a Mandelbrot Set—a recursive set in which the whole consists of the infinite replication of parts. The program allowed one to zoom in on any part of the graphically represented set and see essentially the same pattern with which one started. It struck me as a fantastic example of something (but I just didn't know what). A second stage in the development of the idea was my noticing the evolution of my kids' computer and video games as designers increasingly used fractals to enrich the details of their animation. On the cathode-ray tubes, at least, whole worlds with mountains, waters, trees, rocks, walls, and castles were being created by fractals: graphic chunks of recursiveness. The startling point was that the more the animators generated the landscapes mathematically, the more realistic these landscapes looked.

This recurring interest in recursiveness itself started to connect with something I had learned decades earlier from my first professor in Japanese philosophy and culture, Robert J. J. Wargo, then at the University of Hawai'i. He advised me as a novice in the language, thought, and culture to pick one specific area and fathom it as deeply as possible. The more deeply I understood that one area, he told me, the more I would see connections with everything else in Japan. By this process I would eventually gain significant understanding of the whole culture— something I could not do if I tried to learn the whole culture all at once at some superficial level with hopes of gradually deepening that knowledge. Wargo's advice proved to be immensely helpful. Only as I started to think about the recursive character of culture, however, did I see why his advice worked so well.

And this brings us back to the image of the two recursive trees in the Introduction. Where did it come from? Toward the end of the whole project, I had pondered how to write a brief introduction that would put the reader into the right disposition for understanding what I was going to do in the rest of the book. I was looking for the most succinct and intuitive way to formulate the notion of cultural recursiveness and its pertinence to issues of cultural comparison. At the Caribou Coffee Shop on Lane Avenue in Upper Arlington, Ohio, I looked up from my laptop out the window and saw two maple trees down the street. The animators' fractal landscapes, Bob Wargo's advice, the Mandelbrot Set, and the articles I had read in such places as the *Scientific American*—all of these phenomena and many more overlapped in such a way that the diagram was born. The real trigger for the idea came, however, from the living trees down the street, not from dead trees making up the pages of a book. But how do I cite this source bibliographically? Should I collect DNA samples so the Library of Congress can work up a unique call number for each tree?

Working with the tree diagrams also led me to remember Don Ihde's little gem, *Experimental Phenomenology: An Introduction* (New York: Putnam, 1977), a book I have used in teaching basic courses on phenomenology. By using diagrams like Figures 6 and 7 as well as gestalt pictures like Figure 4, Ihde managed to explain a wide range of phenomenological terms and concepts. My use of "acculturation" as the process by which an orientation becomes second nature directly relates to the phenomenological term "sedimentation," of which Ihde's book makes fruitful use.

What about the very idea of cultural orientation? Whence did it arise? As explained in chapter 1, the problems of cultural comparison and cross-cultural communication came to my attention through my study of Asian philosophy in graduate school. Trying to get a handle on the cultural differences I was encountering, I read the classics on this question available to me at the time. These classics included the three volumes edited by Charles A. Moore—*The Indian Mind: Essentials of Indian Philosophy and Culture* (Honolulu: East-West Center, 1967), *The Chinese Mind: Essentials of Chinese Philosophy and Culture* (Honolulu: East-West Center, 1967), and *The Japanese Mind: Essentials of Japanese Philosophy and Culture* (Honolulu: East-West Center, 1967)—as well as Hajime Nakamura's *Ways of Thinking of Eastern Peoples: India, China, Tibet, Japan,* rev. ed., translated by Paul Wiener (Honolulu: East-West Center, 1964), and F.S.C. Northrop's *The Meeting of East and West: An Inquiry Concerning World Understanding* (New York: Macmillan, 1946). Such interests in philosophically understanding cultural difference dated back to the 1930s. Unfortunately there was a plethora of other works written under a similar theme at around that same time, but their intent was different—namely, to support an ethnocentric ideology for claiming one's own culture, race, or ethnicity as superior to others. Such works were obviously feeding into various nationalistic, militaristic, racist, or ethnic agendas. Think of the opening of Hitler's *Mein Kampf,* for example.

Of course, Moore, Nakamura, and Northrop were not of that ilk. Moore was the philosopher who had established in Hawai'i the initial East-West Philosophers' Conferences with the hopes of bringing together thinkers from around the world to discuss broad humanistic concerns. Nakamura was a scholar of Buddhism who hoped to understand how that religion changed as it moved from one culture to another (India, Tibet, China, Japan). Northrop was a Yale philosopher who also taught in the Law School and was interested in international negotiations. By the 1970s, however, the whole enterprise of analyzing cultural ways of thinking became a target for criticism by anthropologists, political historians, and sociologists. In literary and theory circles, this critique led to the concern that all such enterprises were inherently "orientalist"—categorizing cultures as "other" in ways serving one's own cultural, economic, and political agendas. Along with the writings of "national spirit" fanatics from various countries, the writings of Moore, Nakamura, and Northrop were marginalized. But the scholarly pendulum is beginning to swing back. Global economic, political, and military contexts demand a deeper understanding of cultural difference. At the same time, issues of pluralism and diversity, even within single nations, are also of immediate relevance, as we see in influential books like Charles Taylor's *Multiculturalism and "The Politics of Recognition": An Essay,* edited by Amy Gutmann (Princeton: Princeton University Press, 1992).

The philosophical project of assaying the relation between culture and thought in national cultures has again become the focus of several important works. With the reentrance of China into world affairs, sinologists have led the way this time. Good examples of trying to understand the differences between traditional Chinese and traditional Western modes of thinking and valuing include David L. Hall and Roger T. Ames, *Anticipating China: Thinking Through the Narratives of Chinese and Western*

*Culture* (Albany: SUNY Press, 1995), Henry Rosemont Jr., *A Chinese Mirror: Moral Reflections on Political Economy and Society* (La Salle, Ill.: Open Court, 1991), and Chad Hansen, *Language and Logic in Ancient China* (Ann Arbor: University of Michigan Press, 1983). It would be interesting to see how the insights of these scholars can be interpreted in light of the intimacy/integrity heuristic. How has Chinese culture negotiated intimacy-dominant and integrity-dominant orientations throughout its philosophical history? What is happening today as China is culturally pressured to adopt European notions of economy and politics? The same type of question can be asked of other Asian cultures as well, especially in comparison with Western philosophical traditions. In this regard, anthologies concerning various Asian traditions in comparison with the West might be a good starting point. See, for example, Gerald James Larson and Eliot Deutsch (eds.), *Interpreting Across Boundaries: New Essays in Comparative Philosophy* (Princeton: Princeton University Press, 1988). Moreover, Roger T. Ames, Wimal Dissanayake, and I edited a series of three books of this nature: *Self as Body in Asian Theory and Practice* (Albany: SUNY Press, 1993), *Self as Person in Asian Theory and Practice* (Albany: SUNY Press, 1994), and *Self as Image in Asian Theory and Practice* (Albany: SUNY Press, 1998).

When invited to deliver the Gilbert Ryle Lectures, I reflected on my connection to the work of this great British analytic philosopher. In my sophomore year at Yale I had enrolled in Ross Thackwell's Directed Studies Seminar on the history of Western philosophy from Hegel to the present. For that course I had written a term paper comparing the epistemologies of Gilbert Ryle in his *Concept of Mind* (New York: Barnes & Noble, 1949) and Michael Polanyi in *Personal Knowledge: Towards a Postcritical Philosophy* (London: Routledge & Kegan Paul, 1958). As I thought about this experience three decades later in 1997, I realized that Ryle had represented a good model for an integrity-dominant epistemology and Polanyi (at least in most respects) a model for an intimacy-dominant epistemology. Hence my circles of interdependence leading to the integrity/intimacy distinction include that sophomoric project. This realization surprised me a bit, but it did not bother me. Although we generally use the term "sophomoric" in a deprecatory sense, I have often found the questions of college sophomores philosophically refreshing— free of the rigidified learning regimens of high school and not yet acculturated into the unquestioned assumptions of a scholastic discipline. Sophomores can boldly ask, "why do you assume that?" or "how is this

important?" or "isn't that contrary to common sense?" Just as Sōtō Zen
Buddhism urges its students to return to the "beginner's mind," we
scholars might benefit from going back, at least occasionally, to the
"sophomoric mind." Perhaps even as a college sophomore I had had a
hunch that the differences between Ryle and Polanyi were good examples
of something; I just did not know of what.

Another event from that seminar intersects with this book. In Thackwell's seminar I encountered for the first time, both in writing and in person, the philosopher Brand Blanshard. Blanshard had retired from Yale
some years earlier, but he was still around in New Haven where he unof-
ficially had an affectionate title: The World's Last Living Rationalist.
Thackwell had us read Blanshard's *Reason and Analysis* (La Salle, Ill.:
Open Court, 1973) and then invited the retired philosopher to visit our
class. Around the room we posed various criticisms of his work. In each
case, Blanshard listened patiently and thoughtfully. Then he would begin,
"Do you mean..." followed by an extraordinary clarification and enhancement of what we had said. Our chests would expand with pride as
we heard our half-baked ideas fleshed out into rock-solid philosophical
positions. He would even note how what we had said was like the ideas
of some great philosopher from the past. Then he would follow with
"I've thought about that position and it is wrong. Here's why..." After
a few minutes, all that was left of our rock-solid critiques was rubble.
From this experience, both intellectual and affective, I learned firsthand
from a master the value of taking a few basic assumptions and thinking
them through into a comprehensive position. Only then can one fairly
evaluate whether they are true in any important sense. This procedure
probably goes against human nature. (Or is it acculturated second nature?) It is tempting to jump to negative critiques of philosophical anath-
emas without first figuring out what the disfavored position actually
entails and why some sensible person might hold it. Yet as Blanshard
demonstrated for his apprentice philosophers, however tempting this may
be, it is not good philosophical praxis. I have tried to give my analysis of
both the intimacy and integrity orientations this kind of sustained attention to see exactly where they lead without too quickly jumping to the
question of which is true and which false. By doing so, I ended up changing my very understanding of what "true" or "untrue" might mean, realizing that their relationship with cultural orientations is by no means
obvious.

In that same seminar, incidentally, we also read Blanshard's extraordinary little monograph, *On Philosophical Style* (Bloomington: Indiana University Press, 1954). In it he attacked obscurity in philosophical writing. Blanshard demonstrated that if we recast convoluted, obscure philosophical paragraphs into clear language, many apparently profound assertions turn out to be either trivially true or blatantly false. It was a fine essay to read in a course that had begun with Hegel. It might be equally relevant to many contemporary works of philosophical and critical theory that pass off convoluted syntax or jargon as indicators of profundity. In fact I learned that rendering the profound into something intelligible requires considerable labor—and it is the task of the writer, not the reader, to do most of the work. So I have tried to learn from Blanshard's argument and his own literary example, as well as from other philosophers like him. If Blanshard could have read this book, he would very likely have disagreed with it. But I hope he would have found it generally clear.

What can I say about the origins of the concept and term "intimacy"? As explained in chapter 1, the concept arose from my trying to understand and then teach Japanese culture—in particular, Japanese philosophy. I needed to get a handle on the subject, something both I and my audience could use to grasp the way of thinking behind much Japanese philosophizing. I went to visit TAMAKI Kōshirō at his home in Tokyo to ask him some questions about the philosophy of Kūkai, the founder of Shingon Buddhism in early ninth-century Japan. I had sensed that Kūkai was pivotal in the development of Japanese thought, but I was not sure how. I figured Tamaki would know. Tamaki was one of Japan's premier scholars of Buddhism and I especially appreciated his insights because he was so well versed in Western as well as Asian thought, all of which he read in the original languages. Furthermore, his personal spirituality grounded his interest in how philosophical ideas relate to practice. This topic too intrigued me, and it was through Tamaki's introduction that I encountered YUASA Yasuo, a philosopher I will discuss later.

My visit with Tamaki, as usual, was enlightening on many levels and I began to get a new, more holistic grasp of Kūkai's extraordinarily rich and complex philosophical system. I had finally got it in a fundamental sense so that further study would simply be a matter of filling in details. Riding back on the train to my hotel, I found that my thrill of the insight started to shift into a concern for how I could possibly explain this system to someone else—especially to someone who did not have access to the vast web of Buddhist ideas and practices on which Kūkai drew. I needed a heuristic for explanation. Then I noticed a young Japanese couple, probably college students (sophomores?). In the rather crowded train, they were standing close to each other and saying almost nothing, perhaps a few words here or there. They were, however, suggesting volumes about their intimate relation through their every look, every gesture, and every meager word. Their style of expression, it occurred to me, was remarkably like the way Kūkai described the cosmos as Dainichi Buddha's stylized, esoteric self-expression. I do not think at this point I had quite found the word "intimacy." But from this experience, it would only be a matter of time. What is the bibliographic citation for *this*? Is it Kūkai's collected works in Chinese? Is it Tamaki's essays related to Kūkai's concept of *hosshin seppō* (which means something like "the cosmos as the Buddha teaches the true teachings in all things")? How do I reference the young lovers (names unknown) on the train?

Some readers may believe my not employing footnotes runs the risk of ignoring the crucial influence of intertextuality. Some critical and literary theorists have noted that texts are responses not only to the world but, at least as important, to the way the world has been articulated in earlier texts. Of course, I generally agree with this sense of intertextuality; it is a way to recognize cultural context. (There is, by the way, a stronger position of intertextuality which claims there is no "world" at all, only texts. I find this position untenable. Depending on how one defines "text," the position seems to be either trivially true or blatantly false. To explain further at this point, however, would be too great a digression.) I accept the idea of intertextuality when I realize that even by writing in English, I am necessarily resonating with other texts written in English (or translated into English) before me. Furthermore, there are ideas and terms from texts in other languages that I "translate" into my own English writing. I respect this interdependence and am grateful that the words and concepts I employ have been used by others before me (perhaps in a better way). Does the standard, integrity-dominant form of bibliography really give an adequate picture of this intertextuality? Such a bibliography would present books as a list of discrete entities surrounding this study and relating to it. This is an integrity model of the reality of the situation: the books exist as independent entities shelved in some library and only relate to my book in an external way as I forge their interconnections. According to this way of thinking, the intertextuality is environmental: the books stand around me as the circum-stances in which my book is centered.

From a more intimate way of conceiving intertextuality, this environmental account, however true, misses the point. As I have suggested, the books in my intimate bibliography do not surround me; instead they are part of me. The books—indeed not the books but my *reading* of the books—belong with me, not to me. They are part of my interdependent identity. I am at home with my books and they with me. Hence an intimate bibliography is ecological, not environmental. It is a blueprint of home. Such a bibliography cannot isolate the books from the circumstances of my reading them and from the occasions when their ideas— whenever they might have been first read—finally hit home. It would be strange to claim, for example, that those books by Ryle and Polanyi were direct sources for this book. They only assumed this function when, thirty years after I read them, the invitation to deliver the Ryle Lectures gave me the opportunity to reflect on my own relation to Ryle's writings in the context of the material in this book. In this context I discovered an overlap that already existed, one of which I might otherwise have been unaware. As I have shown, there have been other occasions of ideas hitting home: working with masters of my craft as an apprentice, observing young lovers on a train, having informal conversations, seeing trees down the street. If two works interrelate intimately, there are always more circles at play in this interdependence than the books themselves. The common integrity-dominant bibliography obfuscates this point.

I have intended this book, as I have noted repeatedly, to be a heuristic. I invented it as a tool for organizing, interpreting, and engaging in the act of philosophizing when working across cultures (in the broadest sense of the word). How, then, can this tool be best used? The test of a heuristic tool is not its truth, but its function. When I get my hands on a new tool, I am most anxious to try it out on the tasks at hand. I am not so interested, at least initially, in delving into its historical origins. If I am interested in this information I can read about it in a book dealing with the subject. I don't need this information to use the tool, and I can only fully evaluate its design if I use it. When given too much information about a tool, in fact, I often feel hampered, rather than nurtured, in my creativity. I don't want someone to instruct me on all the possible applications of a screwdriver, for example. One of my favorite tools is an old, beat-up screwdriver hanging handily on my garage wall. I use it for myriad jobs: opening a paint can, stirring paint, prying apart items glued or nailed together, lifting a dollop of putty from the can, temporarily wedging something open, fishing around in short pieces of pipe to break up obstructions or to snag a piece of misdirected jewelry, chiseling wood where there is too much adjacent metal to risk ruining a finely honed wood chisel. In short, I might use it for almost anything but driving screws. (Its battered edge has long ago lost its utility for that.) So much for remaining true to the creator's original intent. Yet I am deeply indebted to the genius who designed this screwdriver. I look at it—varnish worn from most of its wooden handle, flecks of old paint stuck in its indentations, the shaft just a wee bit bent, the edge dulled and nicked, and even a drop or two of my dried blood here and there—and I cannot help but smile. Certainly it is one of my favorite tools.

Of course, I have complex hand and electrical tools that did come with booklets of instruction I appreciate. The booklets explain how to use the tool effectively and, very importantly, what *not* to do with it if you want to avoid bodily harm. And depending on the kind of tool—a handheld electric rotary tool, for example—there is also a section suggesting some of its uses: trimming ceramic laminate edges, woodcarving, cutting embedded nails at the surface, drilling, boring, mortising, edging, grinding, polishing, and so forth. The list is not meant to be exhaustive. Instead it provokes the users' own creativity in solving problems important to them. In following my occasional use of the heuristic in this book, readers have, I hope, acquired some practical wisdom in using the tool. So, no more need be said about that. But the other two functions of the instruction book may still be relevant: the warnings and a list of possible uses. That is: I should probably say something about how to avoid philosophical harm, how not to abuse the heuristic tool, and to suggest some materials on which the heuristic tool might be used. For the latter purpose, I will refer to other books—not as a list of sources, not as a list of "authorities" (heaven forbid), but as a friendly suggestion of how I, the inventor of the tool, have found it useful in dealing with certain materials. Let us begin with three warnings. I have already noted most of these caveats throughout the book, but authors of tool instruction manuals (or their attorneys) seem to find it valuable to present the major warnings in a list. So I will do so now.

Warning 1: Certainly no culture or subculture fits the intimacy or integrity orientation perfectly. It is especially dangerous to apply the heuristic tool to broad phenomena—for example, to claim that "Japanese culture is an intimacy culture" or that "American culture is an integrity culture" or that "women form intimacy groups and men form integrity groups." Such characterizations, unless carefully and extensively qualified, modified, and situated, lead to orientalisms, essentialisms, and relativisms furthering the cause of controlling or ignoring, rather than engaging, the other in discourse. In dealing with real rather than theoretically constructed cases, the heuristic of the intimacy/integrity orientations will help one to analyze, think through, and sometimes function in specific contexts within these real cultures or subcultures. That is: to understand and to engage, it is important to recognize and identify the "language" of the descriptive, persuasive, and normative discourse in a case. This is how the book's heuristic tool is most safely used.

Warning 2: The thought experiment in this book suggests that if one orientation is authoritative in a certain cultural context, it will probably affect the whole descriptive and prescriptive discourse in that context. That is: if one advocates and operates within one orientation's epistemology or metaphysics, there are direct implications for discourse in ethics or politics. Suppose I advocate an intimacy-oriented epistemology. As a consequence, the structure of this discourse will make it difficult or even impossible to advocate persuasively, say, individual moral responsibility or inherent individual rights. To put the problem pithily, I cannot intimately know the integrity assumed in a claim for individual responsibilities or individual rights. Why? Because such responsibilities and rights only appear in an integrity orientation. To know I have such rights commits me to an integrity form of epistemology.

Thus if I am committed to an intimacy-dominant form of epistemology and want to argue politically in defense of something that would otherwise be called "*knowable* rights," I must relinquish explicit references to "rights" entirely. Instead I must develop within my discourse a persuasive political argument for something that would functionally have the same effect within the intimacy-dominant culture that a recognition of human rights would have in an integrity-dominant culture. The discourse might shift, say, from the independence of rights to the nature and value of interdependent human relatedness.

The warning, then, is this: it is philosophically self-defeating to mix-and-match epistemology, metaphysics, analysis, persuasive rhetoric, aesthetics, ethics, and politics from different orientations. Such philosophical enterprises link only within a single orientation. To overlook this structure would be comparable to saying that I will continue to speak in English, but from now on, like a speaker of Japanese, I will place the verb at the end of the sentence instead of the middle. I myself might know what I am saying, but others are likely to think I am at least a little crazy and certainly too unintelligible to follow in conversation. The possibility of true engagement would dissolve. Bi-orientationality entails not only complete fluency in both orientational modes but also an accompanying realization that one must engage in only one mode at a time.

Warning 3: The intimacy/integrity theory of cultural orientations does not entail philosophical or even cultural relativism. If I truthfully say in English "It is raining" or in Japanese *"Ame ga futte iru,"* the value of what I say depends on the actual weather at the time, not in what language I say it. *How* I say it, however, differs in the two languages. The English has a distinctive "it" that does not correspond to anything in the Japanese sentence. If I want to analyze what the "it" might mean or why it has to be in the sentence (as some philosophers of language in the West have in fact done), the example has to be in English. The issue itself cannot come up in the Japanese-language context. Analogously, my claiming that the concept of innate, individual human rights does not arise in the intimacy orientation means simply that the orientation has nothing informative or normative to say about it. To return to the closing discussion in chapter 6, it is like trying to talk about the young woman's ear while being in the gestalt of the old woman. The concept's discussability or analyzability, not its truth, is relative to the cultural orientation. Presumably the old woman does have a left ear, but the gestalt has no way of focusing on it.

Now let us consider some materials on which this heuristic tool of cultural orientations might be handy. Some of these works I know better than others. Indeed, a few I have not really read at all. I simply know of them or have skimmed through them because of a recommendation from a student, colleague, or friend. It is as if I have brought these books home into my intimate locus but have not yet decided exactly where they belong. If we think of such books as materials on which to work—rather than parts of a completed project—they have a rightful place here.

As implied in a few places within the book, one might use the heuristic to explore the transition from premodern to modern philosophical modes of thinking in the West. To what extent is it helpful to think of premodern Western thought as intimacy-dominant and modern Western thought as integrity-dominant? For exploring such a question, one might begin with John Herman Randall's classic *The Making of the Modern Mind: A Survey of the Intellectual Background of the Present* (Boston: Houghton Mifflin, 1940). For studies more in tune with the questions of our time, good candidates for further reading are Susan Bordo's *The Flight to Objectivity: Essays on Cartesianism and Culture* (Albany: SUNY

Press, 1987), Charles Taylor's *Sources of the Self: The Making of Modern Identity* (Cambridge, Mass.: Harvard University Press, 1989), and Stephen Toulmin's *Cosmopolis: The Hidden Agenda of Modernity* (New York: Free Press, 1990).

If it turns out that the transition from premodern to modern Western philosophy was often a swing from intimacy-driven to integrity-dominant forms of philosophizing, would postmodernism be a swing back toward intimacy? To begin thinking about this issue, one might read some of the foundational works heralding a postmodern form of philosophizing such as Elizabeth Deeds Ermarth's *Sequel to History: Postmodernism and the Crisis of Representational Time* (Princeton: Princeton University Press, 1992), Michel Foucault's *The Archeology of Knowledge,* translated by A. M. Sheridan Smith (New York: Pantheon, 1972), and Richard Rorty's *Philosophy and the Mirror of Nature* (Princeton: Princeton University Press, 1980).

Some philosophers have reflected profoundly on the nature of rationality itself and its historical manifestations in Western thought. Does the heuristic of intimacy and integrity add any dimension to such reflections? Two important works on this topic in recent years include Alasdair MacIntyre's *Whose Justice? Which Rationality?* (Notre Dame: University of Notre Dame Press, 1988) and Stephen Toulmin's *Return to Reason* (Cambridge, Mass.: Harvard University Press, 2001).

Does the construction of gender in American culture result in different "ways of thinking" that can be illuminated in light of the intimacy/integrity heuristic? How have integrity-dominant models of knowledge been emphasized in the West and how has gender construction attributed these models to "masculinity"? There are many books addressing this issue in ways that may be helpful in grappling with such questions. Highly regarded efforts include Lorraine Code's *Rhetorical Spaces: Essays on (Gendered) Locations* (New York: Routledge, 1995), Patricia Hill Collins' *Black Feminist Thought: Knowledge, Consciousness, and the Politics of Empowerment* (London: HarperCollins, 1990), Carol Gilligan's *In a Different Voice: Psychological Theory and Women's Development* (Cambridge, Mass.: Harvard University Press, 1982), and Genevieve Lloyd's *The Man of Reason: "Male" and "Female" in Western Philosophy,* 2nd ed. (Minneapolis: University of Minnesota Press, 1993).

The intimacy orientation highlights the importance of incarnate, self-imposed discipline as the praxis for achieving insight. The book most influential on this part of my discussion, including the characterization of such knowledge as "dark," is YUASA Yasuo's *The Body: Toward an Eastern Mind/Body Theory*, edited by Thomas P. Kasulis and translated by Shigenori NAGATOMO and Thomas P. Kasulis (Albany: SUNY Press, 1987). Yuasa is a contemporary Japanese philosopher who first raised the question of why the theories concerning the mind/body relation in modern Japanese philosophy do not seem to mesh with those of modern Western philosophy. Through many years of conversation with him and through my reading of his works, many of his insights about somaticity, praxis, and acculturation have become so interdependent with my own theories that at times I cannot clearly distinguish "his" from "mine." Other works in English directly linked with Yuasa's theories include Shigenori Nagatomo's *Attunement Through the Body* (Albany: SUNY Press, 1992) and David Edward Shaner's *The Bodymind Experience in Japanese Buddhism: A Phenomenological Perspective of Kūkai and Dōgen* (Albany: SUNY Press, 1985). In recent years Yuasa has been developing a metaphysical theory of *ki* (Chinese: *qi* or *ch'i*) based on evidence from various empirical studies. In many respects, *ki* may be an intimacy-dominant interpretation of what an integrity-dominant account might call "matter/energy." Could this be the basis for a systematic philosophy that bridges evidence from both Western and Asian sources? See, for example, Yuasa's *The Body, Self-cultivation, and Ki-energy*, translated by Shigenori Nagatomo and Monte S. Hull (Albany: SUNY Press, 1993).

Feminist philosophical works can be a gold mine in the search for intimacy-dominant epistemologies, politics, ethics, and aesthetics. Just as important, however, many feminist theories seem to argue from an integrity-driven standpoint—perhaps to engage the discourse in modern Western philosophy on its own, integrity-dominant, turf. To sort out such positions in feminist thought one might begin with anthologies including a variety of feminist philosophers such as Linda Alcoff and Elizabeth Potter (eds.), *Feminist Epistemologies* (New York: Routledge, 1993), or Louise M. Antony and Charlotte Witt (eds.), *A Mind of One's Own: Feminist Essays on Reason and Objectivity* (Boulder: Westview, 1993). For anthologies of feminist aesthetics see, for example, Peggy Zeglin Brand and Carolyn Korsmeyer (eds.), *Feminism and Tradition in Aesthetics* (University Park: Pennsylvania State University Press, 1995), and Hilde Hein and Carolyn Korsmeyer (eds.), *Aesthetics in Feminist Perspective* (Bloomington: Indiana University Press, 1993).

For feminist views on epistemology and the institutionalized praxis of science, three classic works are Sandra Harding's *The Science Question in Feminism* (Ithaca: Cornell University Press, 1986), Donna Haraway's *Simians, Cyborgs, and Women: The Reinvention of Nature* (New York: Routledge, 1991), and Lynn Nelson's *Who Knows: From Quine to a Feminist Empiricism* (Philadelphia: Temple University Press, 1990). For ethics and politics, important studies include Virginia Held's *Feminist Morality: Transforming Culture, Society, and Politics* (Chicago: University of Chicago Press, 1993), Nell Noddings' *Caring: A Feminine Approach to Ethics and Moral Education* (Berkeley: University of California Press, 1984), Susan Okin's *Justice, Gender, and the Family* (New York: Basic Books, 1990), and Iris Marion Young's *Justice and the Politics of Difference* (Princeton: Princeton University Press, 1990).

Having interests of my own in religious studies, the philosophy of religion, and philosophical theology, I can imagine various uses of this heuristic tool in these fields. For example, a recurrent issue in the study of religious ritual (or even religious praxis more generally) is the relation between the practice and claims to knowledge. Does a ritual mean something? Does it teach something? For novices to the field of ritual studies, a good way to see the range of approaches would be to read Catherine Bell's *Ritual Theory, Ritual Practice* (Oxford: Oxford University Press, 1992), Ronald L. Grimes' *Beginnings in Ritual Studies*, rev. ed. (Columbia: University of South Carolina Press, 1995), and Victor Turner's *The Ritual Process: Structure and Anti-Structure* (Ithaca: Cornell University Press, 1969). A problem parallel to the question of whether ritual has meaning can be found in certain religious philosophers and philosophers of religion who wonder whether religion itself is more about knowing or feeling. In both ritual studies and the philosophy of religion, I suspect that the discussion often limits itself to integrity's models of knowing. Scientism's contention that scientific knowledge is the norm for all knowing has too often colored analysis in this area. On the one side are those who have argued that since philosophical claims based on religious praxis are not publicly objective, they cannot have the status of knowledge. On the other are those who claim that since religious praxis does give rise to insight, its claims to knowledge must be on a par with those usually made in scientific contexts. In contrast to these two positions, I suggest that religious thought often develops in intimacy-dominant contexts. Religions do, after all, commonly emphasize praxis, somatic as well as intellectual participation, the formation of intimacy groups, the development of acquired sensitivity, an affective aspect of knowledge, and so forth. If we were to understand religious claims to knowledge as formulated in intimacy-dominant instead of integrity-dominant contexts, the discussion about the nature of these claims and their truth would shift radically.

Furthermore, the nature of certain dissimilarities among religions may come into focus if we keep in mind the difference between intimacy and integrity orientations. Consider, for example, the divergence in the discussion of religious symbols between Protestant theologians like Paul Tillich and Catholic theologians like Karl Rahner. For Tillich—see, for example, his *Dynamics of Faith* (New York: Harper, 1957)—a religious symbol is a sign devised by humans in response to the sacred as one's ultimate concern. When such symbols function most potently, they participate in the power of the thing symbolized, in this case, the sacred. Yet following the "Protestant Principle," which admonishes that human finitude always limits characterizations of the divine infinite, such symbols can be no more than bridges connecting the human and the divine. Symbols, Tillich says, should never be confused with the divine itself. This would be idolatry, in effect, a transgression of the infinity of God. According to general Protestant theological thinking, therefore, the Eucharist can be "with" the nature of the divine Christ or it can be a "remembrance" of that nature, but it cannot *be* the divine Christ. Catholics like Rahner, however, have a different, more intimate, take on the meaning and function of religious symbols. For Rahner—see, for instance, his essay "The Theology of the Symbol" in Gerald A. McCool (ed.), *A Rahner Reader* (New York: Seabury Press, 1975)—the symbol overlaps the human and the divine. It is an aspect of God's nature to express itself symbolically and an aspect of humanity's nature to see these symbols as "explicitations" of God's presence in the world. Hence the Eucharist can substantially be the actual body and blood of Christ since God has made it so. The Eucharist, in this view, is not a human invention responding to an encounter with the infinity of God and establishing a connection between the human and divine. Instead, in the traditional Catholic view, the Eucharist is a holographic focal point through which the inherent connection between the human and divine is discovered. The Eucharist is part of God's self-expression. This comparison between a Protestant and Catholic theology of symbols suggests that the heuristic of integrity and intimacy may be helpful even in sorting out differences among followers of the same religious tradition—in this case, Christianity.

In developing this intimacy-based bibliography, what counts about books is not their mere existence but their relation to my reading of them at a certain time and place in my development. In explaining this, I have sometimes found it essential to explain related people and events. Thus conversations, classroom discussions, computer games, trees, and even unknown people have found their way into the web of interdependencies indicative of intimate thinking. I have also listed some books that may be good material for using my heuristic tool. Not all of them belong with me intimately, but I have a hunch they would be good to bring home. They strike me as examples of something important, but I am as yet unsure of what. Perhaps the heuristic of the cultural orientations of intimacy and integrity will help me find out.

Readers of this work may take the readings in this intimate bibliography as mere suggestions in a user's handbook. The books are simply materials on which the designer thinks the heuristic tool might work. Users of the heuristic should feel free, however, to use the tool on whatever materials they have at home and for whatever task needs doing. Although the heuristic tool may not always work on every problem, so long as the user heeds the three warnings, little damage can be done. And if some readers use the tool in their home as I use my beat-up screwdriver, keeping it close at hand but using it for tasks the designer never foresaw, that too would be just fine.

Thomas P. Kasulis received his doctorate in philosophy from Yale University. In addition to numerous journal articles, he is author of *Zen Action/Zen Person* and co-editor of a series of volumes on the self in Asian theory and practice, the latest of which is *Self as Image in Asian Theory and Practice* (1998). Currently professor of comparative cultural studies at The Ohio State University, Professor Kasulis has served as president of both the Society for Asian and Comparative Philosophy (1988–1989) and American Society for the Study of Religion (1999–2002).

CPSIA information can be obtained at www.ICGtesting.com
Printed in the USA
LVOW071506090613

337689LV00006B/520/A

9 780824 825591